SMART

Skills

Study, Motivate, Apply, Reason, and Test

by Teresa Perrin

SMART Skills

ISBN 978-1-940532-09-7

For more information, contact:
Essential Education Corporation
895 NW Grant Avenue
Corvallis, OR 97330
phone: 800-931-8069

Essential Education provides innovative, effective HSE test preparation and adult
learning programs centered on the learner's needs.
For more information, please visit http://www.passGED.com/educators/.

Table of Contents

*"I am always ready to learn although
I do not always like being taught."*

—Winston Churchill

Introduction

SMART: Study, Motivate, Apply, Reason, and Test

As an adult learner, it's important to be SMART. It's common to hear, "I'm not smart. There's nothing I can do about it." That's not true. Smart can be learned. By learning good habits, study skills, testing skills, and reasoning skills, you can be smart and achieve your goals. There are five SMART components: Study, Motivate, Apply, Reason, and Test.

STUDY

Studying is a skill. Many students never learn to study in school, and as a result they struggle with learning their whole lives. In the section Learn Smart, you will acquire study skills that make learning more successful.

MOTIVATE

Motivation is key to achieving your goals. In the sections Plan Smart and Feel Smart, you will learn techniques to stay motivated. Motivation can make the difference between wishing and achieving.

APPLY

You need to apply your skills to the tasks in your life: work tasks, everyday tasks, learning tasks, and testing tasks. You can't make progress toward your goals without applying the things you learn. Throughout this book, you'll find ways to apply skills to your education and your life.

REASON

The section Think Smart will teach you a strategy for reasoning: Clear Thinking. You will learn how to think through problems thoroughly and make better decisions by looking at issues from multiple viewpoints.

TEST

The sections Test Smart and Answer Smart teach you strategies to improve your testing skills. From time management to understanding directions to staying focused, testing requires a surprising number of skills. Honing your testing skills will make test-taking less frustrating and improve your scores.

Chapter 1

Think smart

A Guide to Clear Thinking for Success

*"A man who does not think
for himself does not think at all."*

—Oscar Wilde

What Is Clear Thinking?

The most important ability that people have is the ability to think. Human beings are able to talk, build cities and cars, and imagine fantastical futures or alternative pasts. All of the things that make us human go back to one thing: thinking. It's what our minds do!

Sometimes we take our thinking skills for granted. Because we think every day, we hardly ever notice our own thought processes. We don't control when or how we think because it's automatic.

Thinking isn't just something we do automatically, like breathing. We can learn to think. We can learn about our own thinking. We can control how we think and consider, and we can think more successfully.

Clear Thinking is the process of thinking well. Through Clear Thinking, you can learn how to approach problems, how to learn new information, how to make good choices. In short, you can learn how to use your own mind to your best advantage.

That's a skill worth learning.

Testing Connection

HSE exams test your thinking skills just as much as, or even more than, knowledge of specific facts. The better your thinking skills are, the easier an HSE exam will be.

How Can Clear Thinking Help You?

Clear Thinking is a skill. Like any skill, it takes a little bit of time and practice to learn it. Why should you take the time and effort to learn how to think more clearly? It has a lot of advantages.

Clear Thinking Helps You Make Good Choices

Every day, we make choices. Some of our choices are as simple as what to have for lunch, but we're also making important choices all the time. Even lunch can be an important choice. Do you want the greasy double cheeseburger and fries, or how about a salad and some fruit? How important is this choice? How will it affect your life, right now and in the future? What are the factors that go into deciding?

The difficulty is that there's no clear answer. You don't need to eat salad and fruit for lunch every day, and there's no magic formula for healthy eating. There are hundreds of choices of what you should eat. You take into consideration how much money you have, what you enjoy eating, what's available, what's convenient, what's healthy, and probably a lot of other factors.

Still, when have you really stopped and thought about it?

Maybe you don't need to stop and think through your lunch choice every day, but if you're not thinking about the choices you're making in life, then you're not in control of your life.

You choose answers on a test, and Clear Thinking can help with that. You also choose a career. You choose how to spend your money. You choose what to eat. You choose how to vote. You choose your goals. You choose a school for your children. All the choices that you make have results, and together they determine a lot of what happens in your life. How do you choose wisely? Do you stop and clearly think through the choices that you make?

Clear Thinking doesn't tell you what to do. It puts you in control, so that you can use thinking tools to improve your decisions. Then, when you've made a choice, it's an informed choice. It's a better choice.

Making better choices make a better life.

Clear Thinking Helps You Avoid Problems and Mistakes

Here's an everyday problem that could happen to anyone:

> You're driving to work and running late when a man rear-ends you at a traffic light. He apologizes, admits it's his fault, and promises to pay for all the damages. He asks you not to go through his insurance company, though, because he doesn't want his rates to increase.
>
> What would you do?

No one can control whether their car is hit. It's something that could happen to anyone, and of course, it's a problem. Aside from being late for work, your car is broken. What can you do?

Well, you have a choice to make. Should you go along with the person who hit your car? It might feel like you're dependent on him for help. After all, how else are you going to get your car fixed? You might be flustered, worried, and in a hurry. If the person promises to pay, it might seem like you should go ahead and do it. You don't want to be mean, and the man might seem nice enough and sorry for what happened. If the situation were reversed, you might not want someone calling *your* insurance. You want to be a good person, a friendly person, a helpful person.

If you stop to think it through, what are the potential consequences? The person who hit your car is a stranger to you. If you help him out, what if he later refuses to pay? Will you be able to go to his insurance company in the future? Do you have photos or a police report? Can you prove what happened? How much more difficult will it be later, if there's a problem? What if the damages are just a lot more expensive than the person thinks? What if he doesn't really have enough money to fix your car? Do you even know that the contact information the man gave you is real?

If you rush into making a decision without thinking it through, you might make a mistake that you'll regret. It could cause a lot more problems in the future, when you're stuck with a broken car and no one to help. If you think things through, you can avoid a lot of mistakes and problems, and Clear Thinking tools are designed to help.

Testing Connection
Good thinking skills help you plan for and study for your HSE exam. Clear Thinking helps you stay on track and take the fastest route to achieve your goals.

Clear Thinking Helps You Approach Problems and Find Solutions

Everyone faces problems and stumbling blocks. Sometimes we don't even know what the problem is. We say that we're unlucky. Nothing ever works out right for us. We can't seem to do anything or get anywhere.

The truth is that we make a lot of our own "luck." When you're faced with an obstacle or problem, what do you do? How do you deal with it? Do you stop to think about it?

Clear Thinking gives you tools that can help you understand problems and find solutions. Nothing can stop problems from happening, but there are any number of ways that you could respond to a problem. You have the power to act and react. You can counter a problem by thinking about it, making a plan, and taking action.

Let's say that you've agreed to help the man who hit your car, and when you get the estimate, he agrees to pay it.

Then, you don't get a check. You have to call and remind him. He's so sorry. He's waiting for a paycheck to come in.

Then, finally, you get a check, and it bounces.

You're starting to think that something's wrong. You can go on struggling to get money out of the man, but who knows how long that will continue?

You can stop and think about it. Use Clear Thinking tools to find out all your options, like going to small claims court or making a claim against the man's insurance. Then, decide on the best option for you, and make a plan to get it done. You can take control of the situation, instead of letting the man who hit your car control what's happening, and Clear Thinking gives you the tools to help.

Clear Thinking Helps You Learn

Learning is a natural part of being human. We start out knowing nothing, and we learn almost everything that we do in life. We learn to talk, listen, read, write, think, eat, drive, work, and get along with people. Many people think of learning as something that you only do when you're young or something that is difficult and that happens by sitting in a classroom, listening to a teacher, or reading a textbook.

That's not true. Learning is something we do all our life, and most of the time we learn by having experiences. We learn by doing. We learn by talking with people. We learn when we do something and it causes a reaction.

The more you learn, the more you can accomplish and the more you can understand all the possibilities that are open to you. That's not just possibilities for your job or school. That includes possibilities for enjoying your life and feeling good about yourself.

If you learn from your experiences, then thinking about those experiences helps you learn better and quicker. The same is true for learning from a classroom or a book. The more you ask questions, think about what you're doing, and think about what it means, the more you learn, whether it's in your everyday life or in a class.

The great thing is, the more you use Clear Thinking, the more it becomes second nature. You get into the habit of asking questions and thinking about things from different perspectives. You also accumulate more knowledge and understanding over time, so you have more information to work with when you face new problems and new choices. Your Clear Thinking becomes both quicker and more effective.

Now you have a little bit of background about how Clear Thinking can help you. Really, Clear Thinking is just a set of tools that you can use to make better choices and to think through problems. It's that simple. Are you ready to learn what those tools are and how to use them?

The Six Aspects of Clear Thinking

Problems and issues in your everyday life aren't black and white. They aren't simple, either. It makes sense to look at things in more than one way. The more ways you look at a problem, the clearer you can see the whole picture.

There are six important aspects of Clear Thinking... different ways to look at a problem so that you can see it from all sides. Those six aspects are Attitude, Information, Organization, Reasoning, Alternatives, and Consequences.

Attitude

Attitude is about examining how opinions, values, emotions, and ideals affect the situation. Your own attitude affects how you look at the situation and how you act. Other people's attitudes affect their opinions and how they act. Different attitudes create different points of view, and that can cause conflicts. Considering attitude means considering the human elements of a problem.

Key Attitude Questions:

How do my values, beliefs, and feelings affect my thinking and ideas?

How do others' values, beliefs, and feelings affect their thinking and ideas?

Am I willing to see other perspectives and listen to different ideas?

Information

Information is the body of fact and opinion that is available to you in evaluating the situation. Processing information means evaluating it for relevance and reliability and looking at it in context, to see the big picture and the relevant details.

Key Information Questions:

Do I have enough information, and how can I fill in the gaps?

How reliable and appropriate is my information?

Am I seeing the big picture as well as the details?

Organization

*O*rganization means thinking about how you're approaching the problem and how you're handling your own thinking. To organize your thinking, first identify the main issue. What do you want? What's the problem all about? Then, consider ways to apply thinking skills and order your thinking so you can make sense of your different ideas and how they relate to each other. Organization helps you plan and stay on track. You should organize your thinking process before you start and track your progress while you're considering an issue. When you're done, look back and see how your thinking progress worked or didn't work, and you'll improve your organizational thinking in the future.

Key Organization Questions:

What is the main issue, and what do I really want?

What types of thinking will help, and how can I organize my thoughts?

Can I make a plan to deal with the situation?

Reasoning

Reasoning means examining and being aware of the quality of your thought process. Are you being logically consistent? Is your thought process flawed in any way? Are you looking at cause-and-effect relationships correctly? Are you seeing the big picture as well as the details? Do your conclusions make sense, based on the information?

Key Reasoning Questions:

Are my premises, facts, and assumptions sound?

Do my conclusions follow logically from the facts?

How strong is the support for my conclusions?

Alternatives

Alternatives means looking at different possibilities, not getting stuck with just one way of looking at something. In making a decision or solving a problem, it means letting go of one point of view and considering different viewpoints and possibilities. It means thinking outside of the box and opening doors to alternatives. It involves understanding traditional approaches and then exploring ideas outside of the traditional. Traditional and innovative alternatives should be evaluated for their merits and how they might work together.

Key Alternatives Questions:

What are all my options, without worrying about whether they're possible or even good ideas?

What ideas have people had in the past?

What new, creative ideas can I think of?

Consequences

Consequences can be either positive or negative, short-term or long-term. They are what happens as a result of the decision, the solution to a problem, or action taken in the situation. In evaluating consequences, it's important to consider how likely each potential consequence is and how good or bad that consequence is.

Key Consequences Questions:

What are all the potential results, good or bad, of my plans?

What are the short-term, long-term, and very long-term consequences?

What consequences haven't I thought of, including consequences to others?

Think of the aspects of Clear Thinking as window panes. Each pane shows you a little bit of the whole picture. Put them together, and you can see what's happening.

Thinking about Attitude

When you look at a problem or issue from the perspective of Attitude, you should examine your own thoughts and feelings about the issue. How are you approaching it? Your attitude is complicated. It's made up of all your emotions and your experiences, and it takes some soul searching to think through your attitude.

! Be wary of your own knee-jerk reactions. Take a moment to put aside what you're feeling, so that you can think about why you feel that way.

! Try to itemize what your feelings are. What past experiences are affecting your attitudes? What important believes and values are affecting your attitudes?

! Now, think about how your attitudes affect your approach to the problem. Are you unwilling to face the problem? Are you unwilling to recognize other people's ideas or points of view?

! Do you have a "one right way" attitude about the situation? Most situations are complex, and there's not only one right answer. Many times, even if you disagree with others' opinions, you can learn something valuable from them.

! If you have strong emotions or beliefs that conflict with others, try putting them aside to explore what other people are saying. You don't need to give up your emotions or beliefs or values, but don't let them take over.

! Explain to others how important your emotions, beliefs, and values are. Recognize that other people don't have to agree with you, but that doesn't make your feelings and values unimportant. Other people want you to respect their emotions; other people need to respect your emotions, too.

The best attitude to approach learning is one where you recognize your own feelings, experiences, and beliefs, but you're open to learning new things and understanding what others are trying to say. Many times, people think that they already know the answer, so they don't stop to learn new information. Other times, people have strong emotions about an issue and just don't want to think about it.

Still, new information can't hurt you. No one can make you change your opinion or belief. Listening to others, understanding new information or points of view, is always valuable. Thinking about your own attitude makes it possible.

Once you've considered your own attitude, think about the attitudes of others. Every person has a different point of view. The Attitudes aspect of Clear Thinking helps you look at different points of view and understanding why different people and groups believe different things.

You don't have to agree with other people's viewpoint, but it's important to understand why different people have different ideas. Without understanding other people's points of view, you can get stuck at an impasse where no one will listen to each other, and understanding someone's point of view can be the first step toward a compromise.

! Identify the important people or groups of people that have opinions about the topic. Sometimes, this is your family and friends—other people who are affected by the same things you are. Sometimes, it means organizations or groups who are giving you their opinion.

! Identify whose opinion is important to you. Who do you care about? Who is it important to consider? Understanding everyone's viewpoint can be helpful, but it can also help you make important decisions to identify whose opinion matters most to you. Being aware of the viewpoints of important people (like your boss at work, or your spouse at home) can help you avoid conflict and make good decisions.

! Think about the motivations, goals, values, beliefs, and experience of each person or group. What factors go into their point of view?

* Motivations are the reasons why people say, do, or think different things. A company wants to make money when it tries to sell you something or avoid laws that would cost it money. A friend might be motivated by wanting to help you or not wanting to hurt you by telling you something you don't like. Motivations help explain people's actions.

* Goals are end results that people or groups want. An animal shelter's goals might be to prevent unwanted animals from being born. Your spouse's goal might be to afford to buy a boat, retire early, or take a nice vacation. People's goals reflect their desires—what they want—and they affect people's actions.

* Values are what people think are important. We might all think that a college education is a good thing, but some people think it's more important than others. How valuable we think a college education is depends on our experiences and our

culture—the things that make us different from each other. Sometimes values can conflict. If one person thinks it's very important to have low taxes, and another person thinks it's very important to have good schools, those values might conflict. If the city wants to impose a property tax to improve the schools, the people with different values will have different viewpoints.

* Beliefs are things that we believe to be true. Sometimes, beliefs come into conflict with each other. People have different beliefs about what kind of government is best. People have different religious beliefs. People have different beliefs about how to raise children. Beliefs, like values, come from our experience and culture. Sometimes beliefs may be provable as true or false, but often times it's unclear what belief is "true."

* Experience forms our opinions, values, and beliefs. Experts have a lot of knowledge about a topic, and that knowledge affects their opinions. Your friends and family members may have had good or bad experiences with an issue. Sometimes, their experience gives them valuable information. Other times, experiences can be misleading.

It's much easier to judge opinions and actions once you recognize the values, beliefs, motivations, and experience behind them. Once you truly understand different attitudes, you can decide whether to agree or disagree, who to trust, and how to best argue your own point of view.

Thinking about Information

Information is the basis of all our opinions, beliefs, and actions. We respond to things that we know or think are true about the world. That's information.

There is a lot of information to choose from and to understand. We have different kinds of information. We have our own experiences, what we see or hear. We have what other people tell us. We get information from television, radio, movies, and the Internet. We see advertisements and fictional accounts of real events. How can you sort through all the information to find out what you need? How do you know if information is reliable?

! Start out by evaluating what information you need in order to solve your problem or address the issue. You don't need to know every piece of information known to man on the topic, so you need to think about what information is important.

! Think about the information you already know. Where does it come from? Do you remember where you learned it, or do you just remember "hearing it somewhere"? If you don't know the source of important information, you should verify it before relying on it to make a decision. Your memory can easily trick you.

! Learn to find out information. The Internet is a good source of information, but you also need to know who is presenting the information, because not all the information on the Internet is true. What are your possible sources for information? Just a few are government agencies, magazines and newspapers, news shows, books, or non-profit organizations.

! Get the best information possible. Find out who the experts are. If you want information on how to apply for student loans, go to the people who provide the application. If you want information on baking a cake, go to a cookbook or baker.

! Rate information based on how reliable it is and how likely it is. If information comes from a reliable source and seems likely, then it's your most reliable information. If information comes from a source that might not be trustworthy or someone who has an agenda, scrutinize that information carefully. Remember, information you hear from friends isn't necessarily reliable! Urban legends gain popularity because it's easy to believe something a friend tells you, but your friend might not realize that what they're telling you isn't true. If information comes from a source you think is reliable but also seems unlikely or surprising to you, examine it. Take responsibility for what you believe or don't believe.

! Get information from more than one source. Sometimes, a single source is unreliable or just doesn't include information that might be helpful. If a lot of reliable sources agree on information, then you can probably trust that information. Sometimes the information won't be completely clear, and you'll have to use your judgment to decide what's true.

! When information seems to conflict, look at it closely. Is there a detail you're missing? Is some of the information only true in some circumstances? Is some of the information based on new studies or ideas that aren't proven? Is some of the information provided by people who have a motive or agenda that might bias the information?

! Look at the big picture as well as at the details. Try to get an overview of the situation, so you can put your information in perspective.

! Sort out the opinions and the facts. When you're looking for information, you'll find a lot of people's opinions. Opinions can be useful, but they're not the same as facts. An opinion is only as good as the facts it's based on, so when you're evaluating someone's opinion, you'll need to look at the information supporting that opinion.

The information you find will form the basis for your opinion, so it's important to look at your information carefully and get all the information you need before making a decision. Evaluating information is a skill that you can use every day.

Thinking about Organization

Organizing your thinking is important to making progress. What is the main issue or problem? How can you approach the problem? What thinking skills are going to be helpful? How do you know if you're on the right track? Being organized in your thinking and planning can make it easier to understand issues and come to the best conclusions.

! Understand the problem. What is the main issue? Try to put the side issues aside and decide where you need to focus.

! Decide what your goals are. If you don't really understand what you want, it's hard to make progress. Determining what you want can be difficult, but it's an important step. It will help you figure out what's important and what's just a sidetrack.

! Make priorities. What's most important? What is less important? What's not important at all?

! Think about thinking. What aspects of Clear Thinking will help you deal with this problem or issue?

! Organize your thinking. You can use graphics to organize your thinking.

✱ Use a Venn diagram to compare and contrast two different things or ideas:

Venn Diagram

Each circle is for one thing you're comparing.

Apples   Oranges

red
crunchy
eat peel

fruit
sweet
seeds

orange
sectioned
juicy
peel off

Write things that apply to only apples here.

Write things that apply to only oranges here.

Write things that apply to both in the center.

✱ Use a thought web to chart the relationships of different thoughts or
   to brainstorm:

Thought Web

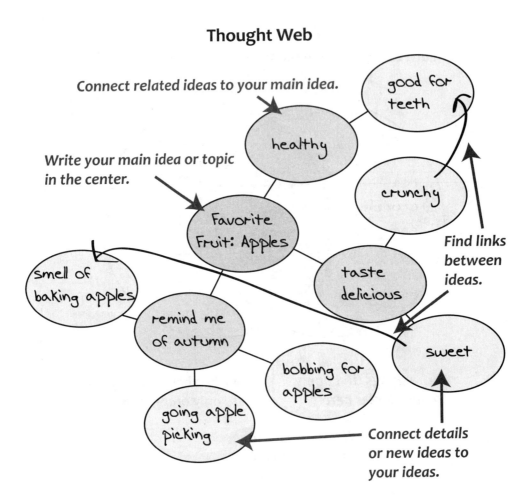

Connect related ideas to your main idea.

Write your main idea or topic
in the center.

Find links
between
ideas.

Connect details
or new ideas to
your ideas.

good for
teeth

healthy

crunchy

Favorite
Fruit: Apples

smell of
baking apples

taste
delicious

remind me
of autumn

sweet

bobbing for
apples

going apple
picking

✱ Use an organizational chart to organize things in a pattern or hierarchy:

Organizational Chart

Arrange a hierarchy, with the biggest idea at the top.

Connect related ideas or details in groups that make sense.

Fruit

Apples

- Red Delicious
- Granny Smith
- Gala
- Golden Delicious

Oranges

- Valencia
- Mandarin
- Navel
- Blood

Testing Connection

Venn diagrams, thought webs, and organizational charts are useful tools for organizing a good written response.

! Make a plan. A plan helps you break up what you need to do into smaller steps and chart a path to get where you're going. You can make an action plan to get things done, but you can also make a *thinking* plan. Which aspects are Clear Thinking are going to be most helpful to you? When will you need them? What will be your goal in using them?

! Track your progress. By thinking about how you're doing, what you've accomplished, whether you're making any mistakes, and whether you've gotten distracted, you can keep yourself moving toward your goal.

! Try improving your thinking process. You can build on what's working for you. Do more of what works best. You can also identify and fix problems with what's not working. Maybe it just isn't a good tactic. Maybe you need an alternative. The more you work at improving your thinking plans, the more quickly and easily you'll figure out what you need to know.

Like many of the aspects of Clear Thinking, Organization requires thinking about your thinking. Thinking about your thinking helps you put your problems or decisions into perspective and helps you avoid making mistakes or going around in circles.

If you tend to procrastinate, getting organized can help you make progress. Make a plan to spend time each day working toward your goal. Organization is the key to discipline: actually sitting down, on a regular basis, and doing the things you want to do. Taking charge requires action. Get organized to take action.

Thinking about Reasoning

To understand Reasoning, it helps to understand different ways of thinking. It's easy to get stuck thinking in a circle. "I have to help out my sister... but if I do that I won't have enough money to get by this month... but she needs my help, I have to do something... but there's nothing that I can do..." It's easy to get stuck with this type of thinking, and it often leads to worry and stress instead of solutions. Once you recognize circular thinking, you can start changing the way that you're thinking.

Three important ways of thinking are linear, or logical, thinking; creative, or innovative, thinking; and intuitive thinking.

! In linear thinking, you move from one idea to the next by a process of logical thought. If this is true, then that must be true. If your sister needs your help, and you don't have the money to help her, then logically you must find a way to help her that doesn't involve money.

! Creative thinking means thinking of new ideas without necessarily being led to them from any logical source. You might use creative thinking to think of ways to help your sister. You could help her find money from somewhere else; you could help her by donating your time. You could help her find ways to save money. Maybe none of these ideas would apply to the situation, but using creative thinking can come up with new ideas.

! Something that's closely allied to creative thinking is intuitive thinking. When you're making choices, do you jump to conclusions because they seem right? Sometimes your intuitions can be helpful, like if you see a man on the street corner while you're walking at night and your intuition says he might be dangerous. Other times, our intuitions mislead us, so it's important to be aware if you're coming to a conclusion through intuition or through logic.

Logical reasoning is really about linear thinking, getting from one place to another step by step. Creative and intuitive thinking can help you in many ways, but linear thinking is where you check yourself, to make sure you're making good choices.

When you reason, you start with assumptions or facts, and you make conclusions based on those facts. That leaves a few places to go wrong:

! Wrong assumptions or facts

! Wrong connections between facts and conclusions

! Giving too much certainty to your conclusions

Facts or assumptions are the *support* for your conclusions. You need to make sure that your support is reliable and true, otherwise all your conclusions could be wrong. That means making sure that you have good information. It also means being aware of what your assumptions are. What are the reasons for your conclusions? What are you basing your findings on? Try to figure out all of your assumptions, because there may be some that you take for granted.

Making wrong connections between facts and conclusions is a common problem with reasoning. There are a few important ideas to understand about making connections between facts and conclusions.

! *Cause and effect:* Understand what the cause is and what the effect is. Is there a logical reason why one thing might cause another? Two things might be related, but that doesn't mean one causes the other. Something else might cause both, for example.

! *If this, then that:* Most logic relies on the idea that if one thing is true, then a second thing is also true. Make sure that this relationship is solid, because sometimes it can *sound* true but not always be true.

! *Some relationships aren't reversible:* Just because all mothers are women doesn't mean that all women are mothers. It makes sense! However, sometimes it's easy to accidentally reverse a connection... and it isn't always easy to see it's not true.

! *An example isn't the whole picture:* If the first person you meet when you come to a town is annoying, that doesn't mean all (or even most of) the people in the town are annoying. A lot of the time, a story about something puts it into perspective. One person's account of what happened to her can be more convincing than a lot of statistics. It's important to remember that one person's experience might be unusual, or even not true! You need to look at the big picture.

Once you come to a conclusion, it's important to weigh *how strong* the evidence for the conclusion is. You might come to a conclusion you truly believe in, but you don't have enough evidence to objectively show that it's true. There's nothing wrong with that, but it's important to recognize that your conclusion is really a *hypothesis,* your personal idea about what's happening. You'll need to investigate deeper and look at more evidence to find out whether the idea is true or not.

If you have a lot of evidence for your conclusion, you can think of it as a *theory.* You can't be 100% certain about your conclusion, because you might run across new ideas or new evidence that explain things in a new way. The more evidence you have, the stronger your theory is. Your willingness to always look at new ideas and reconsider what you think will make you a better thinker and decision maker.

QUESTIONS TO ASK TO CHECK ON REASONING:

? Is my thinking flawed in any way?

? Is my thinking really complete, sound, and clear?

? Am I stuck in one train of thought, a replay of how I thought about this before?

? Do I grasp the cause and effect relationships in what I'm thinking through?

? Do my conclusions follow logically from the information I have?

? Could I reach a different conclusion from the information?

? Is there another way to interpret the information?

? What am I taking for granted? What assumptions am I making?

? Am I seeing the whole picture? Am I focusing only on a few details?

? Is my conclusion a theory, backed by evidence, or a hypothesis that I want to investigate?

Thinking about Alternatives

Alternatives are choices and options that you have. It's easy to get stuck thinking that you don't have any choices, or that there are only one or two things you could do. Usually, you have more choices than you think.

Thinking about alternatives usually involves creative thinking. Your main goal is to break out of the mindset that you only have a few options and think of as many choices as you can. That means doing some brainstorming.

! Identify the choices that you have to make. Where do you have the opportunity to brainstorm for ideas?

! Do a little research. Find out what other people have done. What are the traditional ideas? What do the experts do? Start off with some background on alternatives that other people have thought about or tried.

! Sit down to think of new ideas. Don't worry about the details. Don't worry about whether the ideas will work or not. It isn't about only coming up with good ideas. This isn't about which idea you'll choose. It's about thinking of as many ideas as possible.

! Don't accept or reject any ideas. Thinking "that's the one!" will get you bogged down in the details and prevent you from thinking of any more ideas. Thinking "that won't work!" is just as bad. Even a bad idea can lead you to something new you haven't considered.

! Write down as many ideas as you can. If you have a friend who can help you brainstorm, brainstorming with someone else can help you generate even more ideas.

! You can organize your ideas in a list, in a web, or all over a sheet of paper. Doodle if you want, but get as many ideas as you can.

! Try brainstorming in a few sessions at different times. Take breaks when you run out of ideas.

! Try to come up with new ideas instead of just variations of the same ideas.

! Don't only consider the things that you want to do. Also think about things that seem like they're too hard.

After you've thought of as many possible alternatives as you can, you can narrow down your choices. Consider each idea, and choose the one that seems best.

Thinking about Consequences

Consequences are the results, good or bad, of your choices. Thinking about consequences means thinking about the future, and making connections between causes and effects. Actions have many consequences. Some of them are unexpected, but with a little thought, you can predict many of the results of your choices.

! Consider your goals. Your goals are the consequences that you want. The action that you're planning to take should move you forward toward your goals.

! Think about the short-term and long-term consequences of your actions. What will be the results right away, and what will be the results in the future?

! Don't only focus on what you plan to happen. What might be the unexpected results of your actions? What negative consequences can you expect, as well as good ones?

! Think about the big picture. What are the consequences of your actions for your family and friends or other people who may be affected? Do your actions affect society as a whole?

! Weigh the good and bad consequences of your actions. Any action you take has potential consequences.

? Is this consequence good or bad? How good or bad is it?

? How likely is this consequence? Will it definitely or probably happen, or is it unlikely?

? How much risk am I willing to take? What bad consequences are acceptable to me?

Judging the potential consequences of your action depends on your personal values, priorities, and tolerance for risk. Your conclusion may be different from someone else's, but thinking it through lets you control the risks that you're taking.

My Notes

Applying Clear Thinking to Your Life

How do you apply Clear Thinking to a real-life situation? It's as easy as selecting the aspects of Clear Thinking that you need and asking yourself the right questions to think through the problem until you can see it clearly. Here's an example of an everyday issue that anyone might face:

Maria needs to buy a new car.

How can she decide what choice to make?

Attitude

Maria examines her attitude. She hates to buy cars because she feels pushed around by the salespeople. It's something that she tends to put off as long as possible. Last time she bought a car, she just wanted to be finished. The dealer said they had the car she wanted, but when she got there, they didn't have it. She ended up with a car she didn't really want and payments that were too high. She was able to refinance the car, but she's never been happy with it. Now she doesn't want to even think about it, and she's dreading going to a dealership.

By examining her attitude, Maria realizes that her past experiences are making her unwilling to deal with the issue of buying a car. She is afraid of making the wrong choice. She promises herself to try to put her negative feelings aside. She will do research on the car to make a choice she's really happy with, and she promises herself not to let a salesman bully her. She asks her friend Curtis to come with her to the dealership and help her, in case a salesman tries to push her into a deal.

Alternatives

Before Maria starts looking for specific information, she needs to have a general idea of what kind of car she wants. She tries to think of different alternatives of cars to consider. Does she really need a minivan or SUV for her son? Maybe there's something smaller that will help Maria save money and will be easier to drive? Maria even wonders whether she needs a car at all. Would it be possible to avoid the expense of a car, with all the insurance and gas? She could bike some places, and she's even seen bikes with child seats attached to the back. Another option is that she could join a car co-op, where she pays a monthly fee and can take a car out whenever she needs one. Maria thinks about as many alternatives as she can, even if they seem unfeasible or even silly. She realizes that she has more options than she thought. Maria decides that, at least for now, her own car is the best choice, but she wants to consider smaller cars and hybrid cars to help her save money. She also thinks that buying a used car is a good alternative, but she definitely wants one that's not too old and has a warranty.

Organization

When Maria starts considering what car to buy, she thinks about her goals and tries to organize her thinking. She makes a list of all the qualities that are important to her in a car, plus how much of a monthly payment she can afford. She makes a plan that she will first research which cars will suit her needs, and then narrow them down based on what she can afford. When she finds the car she wants, she'll try to locate it and make a deal on the price.

Information

Maria wants information to make a choice about the right car to buy. She needs information about which cars will meet her criteria. She wants a car that's got a lot of safety features and that will easily hold a car seat for her son. She wants to get good gas mileage because she can't afford a lot of money for gas, and she wants a reliable car.

Maria finds some resources for information about cars, such as *Consumer Reports* magazine, where she thinks she'll find unbiased information. She also gets information on specific cars from car manufacturers, such as the listed miles per gallon.

Maria is able to narrow down her search to four cars.

Reasoning

Maria examines the premises that she's made to come to her conclusions. She realizes that she's missed an important point while narrowing down her search for cars. She hasn't thought of the fact that she'll need to bring her mother out to doctors' appointments and shopping since it's been harder and harder for her mom to drive. Her mom has difficulty getting in and out of a car, so Maria decides to get a car that is easier for her mother. That narrows her choices down to two cars.

Consequences

Maria thinks about the consequences of her two car choices. One is a little bit more expensive than the other, but it's a hybrid and uses less gas. She doesn't think that the amount of money she'll save on gas will make up for the expense. Still, what are the other consequences? On the hybrid, she realizes that she'll get a tax credit as well as saving on gas. Plus, the better gas mileage will help the environment. Otherwise, the two cars are pretty similar. Maria finally decides on the hybrid.

Maria has used the tools of Clear Thinking to make a decision.

It's not hard, and with a little practice, Clear Thinking becomes automatic.

More Clear Thinking Situations

" I'm a single mother, and my parents have retired and moved to another state. They're hundreds of miles away. Going out to visit them is too expensive. We just don't have the money, even for one trip a year. Maybe we could do it every other year, but they expect visits two or three times a year. Why don't they come to visit us sometimes? We want to be a family and stay in touch with each other. I just want them to help with that. "

Attitude: The writer's concern is about money, and she feels she's being treated unfairly. Her parents don't seem to understand the situation—they don't see it from her perspective. She doesn't seem to be sharing her feelings with her parents, and maybe they don't realize the financial hardship. The writer should think about why she's reluctant to talk to her parents about money (or why her parents aren't listening), because not talking about it makes the problem worse.

Information: The issue doesn't revolve around information... but perhaps some information is missing. On the writer's part, why don't her parents visit? Are there health reasons or even financial reasons that the writer isn't considering? From the parents' point of view, do they have the information that the writer has about her financial position? Is there information about cheaper ways to travel?

Organization: The writer needs to identify a main goal. What does she want? Probably, she wants her parents to visit more and therefore share the expenses of keeping in touch. Thinking about attitudes and alternatives will probably be most helpful. She can develop a plan to try to talk with her parents about this issue. She could also use organization to help develop a budget for visits.

Reasoning: The writer reasons that visits to her parents are expensive; she is on a limited budget. Therefore, she should not bear all the responsibility for visits. The reasoning is sound as far as it goes but doesn't necessarily give the whole picture. She answers why she doesn't visit more often but not why her parents don't visit.

Alternatives: The writer hasn't thought of a lot of alternatives, such as phone calls, video calls, instant messaging, ways to earn airfare (perhaps a credit card with travel miles), splitting travel expenses with her parents, talking with her parents about the problem… perhaps there are many more. Brainstorming ideas of how to cut the costs of visits, and also how to talk to her parents about the issue, might be helpful.

Consequences: The consequences of the current situation are that the writer seems to resent her parents and that she must tighten her budget to afford visits and calls. Maintaining silence may lead to growing resentment. The writer needs to look at the consequences of approaching her parents about the issue. How might they react? Why is she reluctant to talk with them about it?

"*About a year ago, I started working at a new job. I work in a small office with three other people all day. The supervisor is named Carolyn. I think Carolyn might be mentally ill, with obsessive-compulsive disorder. She's labeled all the office chairs with our names, and even the coffee cups in the kitchen. One time I used the wrong cup, and she threw it away and bought a new one. It's more than just her strange habits, though. She is a little too friendly and talks about having children and a family in a certain way. She hasn't asked me out or said or done anything outright, but it seems like she's got a crush on me. I like my job and don't want a new one. Still, I find myself trying to avoid her, coming in early or late, taking strange lunch times, cowering at my desk. There's nothing I can do.*"

Attitude: The writer needs to look at his reasons for his discomfort. Is there a way he can confront his feelings and become more comfortable dealing with his supervisor? Does he have bad past experiences, or perhaps just no experience with people with mental quirks or issues? Also, from Carolyn's point of view, what is driving her behavior? Since her social interaction skills don't seem normal, perhaps the writer is misinterpreting her behavior, and even if he's not, perhaps talking about Carolyn's point of view would improve the situation. The writer is currently avoiding the issue instead of facing it.

Information: It might be useful to the writer to find out information about OCD (which is commonly misunderstood) and also information about his supervisor. Talking to others who know her better might help calm his discomfort. Also, the writer should find out information about sexual harassment. In case the problems get worse, it's important to know the facts.

*O*rganization: The writer's main goal seems to be to find a way to work comfortably at his current job. He needs to make a plan to deal with the situation. One part of that plan should be to talk with Carolyn, and if he has problems, he should consider talking with someone higher up in the company and with the human resources department. He should also think about finding a new job if he can't improve his situation. Alternatives, information, and attitude are perhaps the most valuable places to start. The writer can make a plan of how to deal with his supervisor and what to do depending on how Carolyn reacts.

*R*easoning: The writer's actions and assumptions are based on his emotional reaction to his supervisor. Carolyn makes the writer uncomfortable, but she is basically just odd and may or may not have a crush on the writer. The writer might benefit from looking at Carolyn more objectively and with less emotional response, which is where getting some information might help.

*A*lternatives: The writer should look for alternative ways to deal with the situation. He could brainstorm ways to talk to and deal with Carolyn, people to talk to at his company about the problem, ways to get information about why Carolyn acts the way she does, ways to create boundaries in the office, and also ways to deal with his own feelings and become more comfortable around Carolyn.

*C*onsequences: By staying in his job, the writer keeps a job he seems to enjoy, but he's limiting his lifestyle by working odd hours and staying in his work area at the office. If he can become more comfortable with, and understanding of, his supervisor, he can probably improve his situation and be happier. He also has legal options if his supervisor's actions qualify as sexual harassment, and he needs to look at the consequences of pursuing a sexual harassment complaint. The consequences of leaving his job might be a less enjoyable or less high-paying job, and he will need to weigh this against the consequences of his present situation.

" A while ago, my grandfather started losing his eyesight, and it seems to be getting worse. No matter what, though, he won't stop driving, and insists he's okay. Every day, he drives somewhere, the store, or to see his friends. I don't have time to drive him around, between work and two young kids, and my mother has passed away, so there's no one to help me. I am so worried he's going to get into an accident, or lose his license, maybe even hurt someone. He's an adult, he's supposed to be responsible. He won't listen to me, though. He still thinks of me as a little girl. "

Attitude: There are two people's attitudes involved in the situation. The grandfather is getting older, but he doesn't want to have to change his behavior and admit there are some things that he can't do anymore. He might not like his granddaughter giving him advice. After all, he thinks of himself as the adult, the one who makes choices and decisions. The granddaughter is worried but feels helpless. She feels like she doesn't have any real way to respond to the situation, and all she can do is worry. It might be helpful for her to start talking about the issue with her grandfather in terms of the future, that sometime down the road he might need to give up driving. Then, she can start a discussion about what criteria would determine whether he can drive or not.

Information: Some information might help with this problem. Knowing the state of the grandfather's eyes (information from his doctor) and how it's affecting his driving might help. Another kind of information that might help is whether there are organizations or alternative transportation for the grandfather. Are there shuttles for seniors? What about public transportation?

Organization: The woman's main problem is that she's worried about her grandfather and wants to deal with the question of whether he can drive. She can come up with a plan to talk with her grandfather about the issue. The woman and her grandfather might also be able to make up a plan for how her grandfather can safely get where he needs to go.

Reasoning: The grandfather's reasoning needs to be checked. He doesn't want to give up driving, but is this just an emotional decision? If the information shows that it's not safe for him to drive, he needs to check why he's opposed to stopping driving.

Alternatives: Thinking of alternatives could help. The grandfather and granddaughter could think of alternative ways for the grandfather to get transportation. They could also try to brainstorm alternatives so that the grandfather doesn't need as much transportation, or so that the granddaughter can adjust her schedule to help more.

Consequences: The grandfather needs to think about the consequences of driving, even if his eyesight is failing. What risks is he taking, to himself and others? What legal consequences could there be? What are the consequences if the granddaughter doesn't address the situation?

My Notes

Clear Thinking Mini-Situations

Now it's your turn to apply Clear Thinking. Try using a few Clear Thinking tools to think through the following hypothetical problems and situations.

Situation 1:

Your doctor tells you that your blood pressure is high, and he wants you to start taking blood pressure medication and managing your diet and exercise.

Attitude: How would you react to the situation? What would your attitude be?

_____

_____

_____

_____

_____

_____

Information: Where would you go to get information? What kind of information would you need?

_____

_____

_____

_____

_____

_____

_____

_____

Organization: What questions would you have? What plan of action would you make?

_____

_____

_____

_____

_____

Other thoughts: What other aspects of Clear Thinking might you use to think through this situation? What other thoughts or ideas do you have?

_____

_____

_____

_____

_____

Situation 2:

You've gotten laid off from your job, and you only have one month's salary in your savings.

Attitude: How would you react to the situation? What would your attitude be?

_____

_____

_____

_____

_____

Organization: What goals would you have, both for getting a new job and for getting by financially? How might those goals conflict?

_____

_____

_____

_____

Information: How can you find out information about financial resources to help you out until you can get a new job?

_____

_____

_____

_____

Alternatives: How many different ways can you think of to look for a new job?

_____

_____

_____

_____

Other thoughts: What other aspects of Clear Thinking might you use to think through this situation? What other thoughts or ideas do you have?

_____

_____

_____

_____

Situation 3:

Y ou have an opportunity to go to a conference on the other side of the country. It would give you a lot of contacts and recognition, possibly leading to new job opportunities. On the other hand, you need to pay for the conference yourself.

Attitude: How would you react to the situation? What would your attitude be?

_____

_____

_____

_____

Consequences: How would you weigh the good and bad consequences of taking this opportunity?

_____

_____

_____

_____

Reasoning: What are the cause and effect relationships you looked at in weighing consequences? What is the thought process you're using to come to your conclusion?

_____

_____

_____

Other thoughts: What other aspects of Clear Thinking might you use to think through this situation? What other thoughts or ideas do you have?

_____

_____

Situation 4:

Your mother has had a seizure and is in and out of the hospital having tests, and she's not allowed to drive. There is no one else in your immediate family that can help, but you also have health issues. Your doctor cautions against too much driving or spending time in hospitals, where you could get sick easily.

Attitude: How would you react to the situation? What would your attitude be?

_____

_____

_____

_____

Consequences: How would you weigh the good and bad consequences of helping or not helping your mother?

_____

_____

_____

_____

Alternatives: Can you think of any alternatives that would allow your mother to get the care she needs while not endangering your own health?

_____

_____

_____

Other thoughts: What other aspects of Clear Thinking might you use to think through this situation? What other thoughts or ideas do you have?

_____

_____

_____

Situation 5:

Y ou've unexpectedly won $10,000 and will have to pay about $4,000 in taxes on the money.

Attitude: How would you react to the situation? What would your attitude be?

_____

_____

_____

_____

Alternatives: What alternative choices can you think of for things you would do with the money?

_____

_____

_____

_____

Consequences: How would you weigh the possible good and bad consequences?

_____

_____

_____

_____

Other thoughts: What other aspects of Clear Thinking might you use to think through this situation? What other thoughts or ideas do you have?

_____

_____

_____

_____

Expanded Clear Thinking Situations

L ook thoroughly at each of these situations and decide what questions and issues are posed. How would you apply each of the aspects of Clear Thinking to the situation?

" I went to my friend's college graduation last June, and I bought a special portrait from a local artist as a graduation gift. Unfortunately, the portrait was not completed in time for the graduation. I let my friend know his gift was late, but now it's been two months. The artist won't respond to me or tell me what's happening. Plus, I put down a deposit on the portrait. Now, I don't know what to do. Should I wait for the gift to be finished or give my friend something else? What should I do about the artist and my deposit? I can't afford to just lose that money."

Attitude:

_____

_____

_____

_____

_____

_____

Information:

_____

_____

_____

_____

_____

Organization:

_____

_____

_____

_____

_____

Reasoning:

_____

_____

_____

_____

_____

Alternatives:

_____

_____

_____

_____

_____

Consequences:

_____

_____

_____

_____

_____

" I think my husband is cheating on me. I found a receipt for dinner at a fancy restaurant from a day that he said he was working late. It was an expensive dinner and drinks. He never takes me out to a restaurant. I have to cook for him every day, and I take care of the house. I never get a break or a date, and it makes me mad that he would take someone else out like this. I'm sure he's having an affair. "

Attitude:

_____

_____

_____

_____

_____

Information:

_____

_____

_____

_____

_____

_____

Organization:

_____

_____

_____

_____

_____

_____

Reasoning:

_____

_____

_____

_____

_____

_____

_____

Alternatives:

_____

_____

_____

_____

_____

_____

_____

Consequences:

_____

_____

_____

_____

_____

_____

_____

" *My community group is trying to start a project for our town to be energy-independent. They're trying to push everyone to participate in 'green' programs, like recycling and installing solar panels. They've got local artists creating sculptures from trash as part of their publicity for all this stuff. They're even talking about building a hydroelectric plant. I'm really concerned about what the costs are going to be and whether it will raise taxes. I want to say something, but it seems like no one wants to hear anything negative. I feel like I can't even express one opinion without being treated like a horrible naysayer who wants to be dependent on foreign oil. I just don't know if I can make such big changes. I mean, they're trying to upset everything about how we get our energy.* "

Attitude:

_____

_____

_____

_____

_____

_____

_____

_____

Information:

_____

_____

_____

_____

_____

_____

_____

_____

Organization:

_____

_____

_____

_____

_____

Reasoning:

_____

_____

_____

_____

_____

Alternatives:

_____

_____

_____

_____

_____

Consequences:

_____

_____

_____

_____

_____

" My daughter is only 15, and I just found out she's pregnant. I don't want her to drop out of school, but I don't want her to give up the baby, either. I want her to let me help raise the baby so she can finish school. She hates this idea. She wants to get married to her boyfriend, who's only 17, and she thinks they can both drop out of school and find work to support themselves. She's threatening to run away, and I don't know what to do. She says that letting me raise her child is worse than giving it up for adoption and that I'm a terrible parent. Sometimes I think she's right! "

Attitude:

_____

_____

_____

_____

_____

Information:

_____

_____

_____

_____

Organization:

_____

_____

_____

_____

_____

_____

Reasoning:

_____

_____

_____

_____

_____

Alternatives:

_____

_____

_____

_____

_____

Consequences:

_____

_____

_____

_____

_____

The best way to learn Clear Thinking is to apply it to real problems in your life. It doesn't matter if the problems are simple or complex. How can you make the best shopping list? How can you budget for your family? How can you decide on the best job? Where should you go on vacation this year? Try applying Clear Thinking to real issues in your own life, because learning through experience that's meaningful to you is the best kind of learning. Use the following worksheets to help you apply Clear Thinking to your own life.

Clear Thinking Worksheets

In many ways, Clear Thinking is about asking yourself questions. Use these worksheets as a guide to ask yourself questions, and find answers, about the situations or problems that you need to think through.

My Own Attitude Worksheet

Do I have any strong emotions about this situation or problem?

_____

_____

_____

What are my worst fears about what will happen? How are my fears affecting my thinking?

_____

_____

_____

Do I have any past experience with this type of issue or problem? How are my past experiences changing my attitude?

_____

_____

_____

Am I open to new ideas or new thinking on this topic? Do I think I already know the answers?

_____

_____

_____

Am I confident that I can take control of the problem or situation? Do I feel like the problems are too big for me to do anything?

_____

_____

_____

Are there outside things confusing the issue? Am I letting other parts of my life interfere with my thinking?

_____

_____

_____

Where do my ideas or beliefs on this subject come from?

_____

_____

_____

Do I get upset or emotional when talking or thinking about this issue?

_____

_____

_____

Do I want everyone to agree with me about the situation? Am I willing to accept that I can't change everyone's opinion?

_____

_____

_____

Is this an issue that I avoid or procrastinate about for any reason? Why?

_____

_____

Attitudes of Others Worksheet

Who are the important people or groups involved in this issue?

_____

_____

_____

Whose opinions and viewpoints are important to me?

_____

_____

_____

What are my own values regarding this issue? What is most important to me?

_____

_____

_____

Are there people or groups who disagree about this issue? What are the different values important to those people or groups?

_____

_____

_____

What types of emotions are generated among different people and groups about this issue?

_____

_____

_____

What are the motives for people or groups who have opinions about this issue? Does anyone have anything to gain?

_____

_____

What are the beliefs of those who have opinions about this issue? Do they have fundamental beliefs about the world that conflict?

_____

_____

What are the ideals of people or groups who have opinions about this issue? What are they striving for in the world?

_____

_____

What are the specific goals or objectives of people or groups who have opinions about this issue?

_____

_____

Am I willing to accept that different points of view can come from different values, and there may not be a clear "right" and "wrong"?

_____

_____

Can I tell the difference between an opinion based on poor evidence or faulty premises and one based on differing values?

_____

_____

Information Worksheet

What information do I already have about the problem or situation?

_____

_____

_____

What information am I lacking? Where is the best place to find reliable information to fill in the gaps?

_____

_____

_____

Have I looked at information from multiple sources, or is all my information from one place?

_____

_____

_____

Have I compared information on both sides of the issue?

_____

_____

_____

Do I have information from good, reliable sources without motives that might bias them?

_____

_____

_____

Do I have information that gives an overview—a "big picture" view—of the situation?

_____

_____

Do I have information that gives me the details that I need?

_____

_____

_____

In the information that I have, what is fact and what is opinion?

_____

_____

_____

Are my own opinions formulated on facts and information?

_____

_____

_____

Am I using any information that is unlikely or surprising? How can I verify that this unlikely information is true?

_____

_____

_____

Do I have any conflicting information? How can I decide which information is true? Am I looking at the conflicting information in detail?

_____

_____

_____

Organization Worksheet

What is my main goal? Is it a well-defined goal?

_____

_____

What is my focus? Am I looking at the big picture or the details, or both?

_____

_____

How can I organize my thinking about this issue?

_____

_____

What way of looking at the problem will be the most useful?

_____

_____

_____

What aspects of Clear Thinking will be the most useful? What order will be most useful?

_____

_____

_____

How can I make a plan to achieve what I want or to make a decision?

_____

_____

_____

Can I use any graphic organizers to organize my thinking, like a thought web or a Venn diagram?

_____

_____

Visually organize your thoughts in a graphic organizer:

How can I keep track of my progress toward my goal?

_____

_____

Reasoning Worksheet

Am I making any intuitive leaps in my thinking?

_____

_____

_____

Am I using linear thinking? Can I use linear thinking to my advantage?

_____

_____

_____

Am I using creative thinking? Can I use creative thinking to my advantage?

_____

_____

_____

_____

Is my thinking flawed in any way? Is my logic complete, correct, and clear?

_____

_____

_____

_____

Am I trapped in a circular loop of thought? Is my thinking leading anywhere?

_____

_____

_____

_____

What are the cause and effect relationships in the situation?

_____

_____

_____

_____

What is the support for my conclusions?

_____

_____

_____

_____

What assumptions am I making?

_____

_____

_____

_____

Do my conclusions follow logically from my assumptions?

_____

_____

_____

_____

Is my idea a *hypothesis* or a *theory*? How strong is the support for my idea?

_____

_____

_____

Alternatives Worksheet

In what areas do I need to think of alternatives? What are the choices that I need to make?

_____

_____

_____

Am I only focused on one or two possibilities? Have I looked at other choices?

_____

_____

_____

Am I too focused on the problems posed by my path, or by one option, to see other possible paths or options?

_____

_____

_____

Do I get too bogged down in thinking out the details of one choice to look at a lot of other possible choices?

_____

_____

_____

Am I only considering things that I want to do or that I think will be easy?

_____

_____

_____

When I'm thinking about alternatives, do I list a lot of options, even ones that don't seem possible at first?

_____

_____

_____

Have I researched what other people have done in the past?

_____

_____

_____

Have I looked into the options that are recommended by experts or professionals?

_____

_____

_____

_____

Have I tried to think of new, creative options that no one has tried?

_____

_____

_____

_____

How can I come up with the most possible options?

_____

_____

_____

_____

Consequences Worksheet

Will my potential actions achieve the goal I'm hoping to achieve? What could prevent my actions from achieving that goal?

_____

_____

_____

What consequences might my actions have that I'm not anticipating?

_____

_____

_____

How many potential consequences can I predict for my actions?

_____

_____

_____

What are the immediate (short-term) consequences of my actions?

_____

_____

_____

What are the future (long-term) consequences of my actions?

_____

_____

_____

_____

How do I place a value—good or bad—on a consequence? How good or bad are the potential consequences?

_____

_____

_____

How likely are the good and bad consequences of my potential actions?

_____

_____

_____

How high is my tolerance for risk?

_____

_____

_____

When is an unlikely consequence worth taking a risk?

_____

_____

_____

Do my actions have consequences for others as well as for myself?

_____

_____

_____

_____

Chapter 2

Plan smart

Setting Goals and Achieving Them

"It takes as much energy to wish as it does to plan."

—Eleanor Roosevelt

What Is a Goal?

What do you want in life? Everyone has dreams and aspirations. Maybe you want a good job and enough money. Maybe you want to buy a house and to give your kids a college education. Maybe you want to get married and have children or to find a job that you really love. Maybe you want security for the future or to be able to retire. Maybe you want to travel and see the world. Maybe you just want to have free time to golf or paint or do what you love. You want to be healthy, and you want to be happy. Maybe you want to have friends and to do something good for your community or for your children.

Most people have a lot of dreams and ideas about what they want. You probably do, too. Some of those ideas are vague wishes for the future. How do you get there?

For a lot of people, dreams are in the future. They're for "someday," and the road to achieving them isn't very clear. Maybe you'll get lucky. Maybe a chance opportunity will come by some time.

The truth is that people make their own luck and define their own lives. You can't change where you're starting, but you can change where you're going.

The best way to get where you want to be is to take action and that means making a goal. A dream, a wish, or a desire can be vague and passing, but a goal is a well-defined idea of something that you want. Once you have a goal, it's not something that might happen in the future. It's something you're working on today, even if it will take a while to get there.

Think about a soccer goal. You have a ball. You have teammates who can help you. On the other side of the field, there is a goal. It's where you're trying to get, and you have specific, definite ideas about it.

! You need to get the ball into the goal.

! You need to get there as quickly as possible.

! You need to play by the rules on the way to your goal.

You've got teammates who can help you, and you've got opponents and obstacles who are going to try to stop you. You know exactly what you're trying to do.

A goal in life is exactly the same. Your goal needs to be well-defined. You need to know what you want and be able to visualize details about it. Your goal is not somewhere you are now; it's somewhere you want to be in the future. It's not something vague; it's something specific. You'll be able to know when you get there because you can identify it or measure it. Your goal is definite.

More than that, a goal is the result of your actions. It's not something that's just "going to happen" to you. A goal is something active that you do for yourself.

Think about a soccer player. He doesn't just hope that the ball will go in the goal or kick the ball aimlessly around the field.

Think about a business executive. She wants her company to make $500,000 this quarter. That's a goal. It's specific. She needs to take action to make it happen. If it's truly a goal, she doesn't just sit by and wait to see how much sales are. She plans advertisements and sales, and she decides where to promote and sell her product. She is running down a playing field toward her goal, just like the soccer player.

The same is true for your goals. Whatever your goal is—to take a vacation to Florida next summer, to get into college next fall, or to have enough money when your child is 18 to send her to college—you're responsible for making your goal happen. You're running down a playing field. Your goal guides you where you're going.

How Do Goals Help?

What do goals really do for us? How do they help us achieve? Everyone has made New Year's resolutions... and had them drift away before the end of January. Everyone has ideas of things they want to achieve and that they don't seem to get closer to, no matter how many years pass.

A goal is not just a New Year's resolution or a desire. A goal is different. It's more specific. It's more permanent. It demands a plan of action from you.

Here are the ways that goals can help you do more than dream about what you want:

A Goal Is Thoughtful

Making a goal is something worth taking seriously. It requires taking the time to define it and to set plans in motion. You're not making a decision on the spur of the moment. You need to sit down and think.

Because you think through a goal, you need to face the question: What do I really want? Forcing yourself to think through and define a goal means that you're owning up to what will really make you happy.

In fact, the most important part of defining a goal is trying to understand what will make you happy and what will give you what you want out of life. It's a difficult question for most people. Still, once you have a clear idea of what you want, you're on your way to a more fulfilling life.

A Goal Is Written

A goal is not something that changes every day. You've put a lot of thought into it. You are committed to work toward it. It's something permanent. Of course, there are goals that are bigger and smaller. There are goals that are easier, and some that are more difficult. There are goals that are short-term and ones that take years. Still, goals are worth taking seriously. Put your goals in place and stick with them.

That doesn't mean your goals can never change, but changing a major goal should be serious business. Think of it like changing the United States Constitution.

The Constitution sets out rules for our country. It wasn't something decided lightly. It's something written, honored, and permanent. Still, it's possible to change the Constitution through amendments. It's not easy, and it shouldn't be. It should be something that requires thoughtful consideration and agreement.

Changing your goals should also require thoughtful consideration. Your goals have meaning. That's why a goal needs to be written.

Writing down your goal gives it a sense of permanency and importance. By writing down your goal, you are committing to it. You are putting it in black and white: This is what you want to achieve. A written goal is more real to you, and that actually helps you achieve it. You're taking your own goals more seriously.

Your goal should be written down and kept in a permanent place. A good idea is to keep a binder where you track your progress toward a major goal. The first sheet in that binder should contain your written goal.

A Goal Has a Plan

Inherent in the idea of a goal is the idea of a plan. A goal is an action item. It's the result that you expect to get to through your strategy. You can't have a goal without a plan, because without a plan, it's not really a goal.

Think of the soccer player again. He knows that he has to get the soccer ball into the goal. That drives the development of plans. That's how soccer teams develop plays. It's why the players run and kick when the game starts.

Goals are action-oriented things. Having a goal will get you moving across the field, and that's really what you want: to get moving. It's the only way to get where you're going!

A Goal Has a Timeline

A goal helps motivate you by setting up a timeframe for what you want. A well-written goal includes a time to achieve your goal. You can't just let time pass and not move closer to your goal because your goal sets time limits.

The biggest obstacle that prevents people from achieving their goals is procrastination. Getting started on a path toward what you want is difficult. Taking the first steps is hard. Why? Because you don't know, for sure, exactly where you should start. Think about taking a class. What's the hardest day? The first day, of course. You have an idea of what will happen and where you need to go, but you haven't experienced it.

Once you start on the road to your goal, once you're actually on the journey, it's easier to accomplish. Getting started is the hardest part, and that makes it easy to put off getting started.

A timeline defines when you need to get started and where you need to be on your way to your goal. If you're procrastinating, you aren't getting where you need to be. Where you can be tomorrow depends on where you are today. To get to your goal, you need to start taking the first steps right away. Your goal's timeline should keep you motivated and on track.

A Goal Has Accountability

Creating a goal means creating a responsibility for yourself. If you adopt a cat, you are taking on the responsibility of cleaning the liter box, feeding the cat every day, making sure it has fresh water, and taking it to the vet. If you create a goal for yourself, you are taking on the responsibility of making the plan, taking action to achieve the goal, and tracking your progress. You can't just ignore your goal. You can't think that it will take care of itself.

What if you don't achieve your goal? You're the one who is responsible. You're accountable to yourself for your success.

Take that accountability seriously.

Make sure that your friends and family are willing to put you to task, to make sure you're staying on track. Make sure that you're willing to be responsible for taking action.

After all, you're doing this for yourself. If you really want to achieve your goal, you will keep track of your progress. You will make sure you're being responsible. You will do what needs to get done.

You wouldn't ignore your children's needs or your family's needs. Are you ignoring your own needs? Those needs are just as important. By being responsible to yourself, you're also helping your family. You're helping improve your ability to care for others. You're helping to improve the lives of everyone around you.

By taking on the responsibility for achieving your goals, you're creating a positive situation. You achieve things that are valuable to you. You are happier in your life. You are better equipped to help your family and friends. You improve life for people around you. Your goals create a brighter future.

My Notes

Types of Goals

Not all goals are the same, and there are different types of goals for different aspects of your life. There are two ways to look at different types of goals, and looking at different types of goals will help you define the goals that you most want to achieve.

Goals for Different Areas of Your Life

Start by thinking about the different parts of your life. You're a whole person, and you have different levels and types of needs. You need food and shelter, but you also need self-expression and relaxation. You need family, friends, and a strong sense of self. You need a career and you need hobbies. In every area of your life, you have things to achieve. You can set goals for yourself in all of these areas.

GOALS FOR YOUR MIND

Don't neglect your state of mind when you're thinking about goals. Do you have a bad temper? That's something that you can work on improving. Are you afraid of failure? Improving your state of mind can help you achieve a lot of other goals.

Are you forgetful? Bad at math? These aren't inherent parts of you that can't change. Even a person's IQ can change over time. There are many ways that people learn and grow, and having goals for your own mental development can help you grow and change.

You can work on being more caring to those around you. You can work on becoming an expert in the local birds in your area. You can work on understanding the political issues that affect you in your life. You can work on learning to resolve conflicts with your family, friends, or coworkers. You can become a better reader, a better writer—a better thinker.

Goals for your mind can be valuable to you in every part of your life.

What ideas do you have for goals for your mind?

_____

_____

GOALS FOR YOUR BODY

Quitting smoking or losing five pounds are fairly common goals. These are goals for your health. Having a healthy body can improve your life, and there is a lot of information to help you achieve goals for your health. If you have specific health issues, you will want to tailor your goals to those issues. Still, anyone can improve his or her health. Consider the following areas to improve your overall health:

! Goals for increasing your activity level and getting more exercise

! Goals for eating a healthy diet

! Goals for getting regular health care and screenings

! Goals for reducing stress

You may want more than just health. You might want to run a marathon or win a tennis tournament. You might have goals for lifting weights or for competing in a beauty pageant. Your goals will depend on your personal desires and priorities, as well as your health. Your body is where you live every day of your life, and so creating goals for your body can be rewarding and fulfilling.

What ideas do you have for goals for your body?

_____

_____

_____

GOALS FOR SELF-EXPRESSION

As long as 30,000 years ago or more, human beings were creating art on cave walls. The need for self-expression is a basic one. Once we're fed, clothed, and sheltered, human beings want to express their emotions, ideas, and points of view. We do it by talking to our friends and family, by decorating our houses, by choosing our clothes, or in any one of hundreds of ways. How do you express yourself?

Self-expression is valuable because it allows us to creatively develop ideas about the world and about ourselves. Some forms of self-expression include:

! Music. You can express yourself through learning an instrument, joining a local choir, or even through collecting records.

! Clothes. What you wear expresses who you are. Whether you're into sewing or shopping, clothing can be your self-expression.

! Decorating. You can design a living space that expresses your aesthetics.

! Crafts. Crafts can be as varied as floral arrangements, creating mosaics, scrapbooking, or building watches.

! Cooking. Food can be creative, expressive, and fun. Whether you enjoy baking and cake decorating, barbecuing, beer making, or just creating a home-cooked dinner, cooking can be an expressive outlet.

! Gardening. You might want to create an elegant outdoor space or grow your own food. You might want to create a community garden or teach your children about making things grow.

! Arts. Sculpting, painting, photography, or drawing helps you express visual ideas.

! Writing. Journal writing, short story writing, blogging, writing papers or articles, and even letter writing can be self-expressive. Writing allows you to formulate ideas and communicate them.

! Speaking. Public speaking and even chatting are ways to express yourself.

! Creating. Writing, music, the arts... they're all about creating. That's not all you can create, though. You can create anything: a business, an invention, a new way to think about science. Creation isn't limited to a few types of arts and crafts, and self-expression isn't either.

Different people express themselves in different ways. Creating goals for self-expression can help you find out more about your own point of view, and it can lead to new paths to happiness and achievement.

What ideas do you have for goals for self-expression?

_____

_____

GOALS FOR SERVICE

Service is an important part of many people's lives. One person can make an amazing difference in his or her community. Service goals can mean volunteering time at community organizations or creating whole new programs to help others.

Service goals aren't only about helping others. People who set high service goals for themselves find that they're empowered. Because they are doing important work in their community, they realize how much they can achieve in life. Because they see the positive affects of what they're accomplishing, they realize how valuable they can be as people.

Many people become involved in service because they see how problems affect their family, their friends, and their own life. If you're setting a service goal, make sure it's something meaningful to you. You'll be more motivated, and you'll have better ideas of how to achieve your goal.

What ideas do you have for goals for service?

_____

_____

_____

GOALS FOR YOUR FAMILY LIFE

Do you want to start a relationship or have children? Do you want to create more family time? Organize a family schedule? Open lines of communication with your children? Improve your relationship with your mother or father? Spend more alone time with your spouse?

Your family life needs care and tending. You can set goals to help you improve every aspect of your life with your family.

Remember, a goal for your family life involves other people. When you're setting goals that involve relationships, it's always best to include others in the goal-making process. Goals for a family can be set together, and family members can help support each other to make sure the goals are being achieved.

What ideas do you have for goals for your family life?

_____

_____

_____

GOALS FOR YOUR LIFESTYLE

Perhaps you want to live in the country, or maybe you want to move to the city. You might want a life where you only have to work 20 hours a week, or maybe you want to be able to retire when you're 55. You might want to be able to go camping three times a year or visit your sister every day.

All of these goals are lifestyle goals. You want to be able to live in a certain way. Lifestyle goals can be important to happiness. Setting a lifestyle goal means defining what type of life makes you most comfortable and happy. It's very personal, depending on your culture, tastes, experiences, and preferences. It's also a type of goal that often affects others close to you: your family and friends.

What ideas do you have for goals for your lifestyle?

_____

_____

_____

GOALS FOR YOUR EDUCATION

Education doesn't stop when you leave school. Improving your education can improve your mind, your self-esteem, your career, and your life.

You have two choices for educational goals. You can pursue *formal education* or *informal education.*

Formal education means getting a degree or certificate through an educational institution, such as a state department of education or a college or university. Formal education may qualify you for more jobs and provide a credible framework for improving your skills. You can achieve a degree or certificate that shows your accomplishment, which can also improve your self-esteem. One of the benefits of a formal education is that schools provide a path for learning. Once you've chosen a school and an educational path, the school will give you a structure for learning, providing classes and instruction.

Informal education means expanding your knowledge and understanding outside of a formal school environment. You can learn on your own and investigate any area that interests you. Informal education can help with your career, but it is often more valuable for personal growth and development. If you're pursuing informal education, you'll need to formulate your own plan and create your own path for learning.

What ideas do you have for goals for your education?

_____

_____

_____

GOALS FOR YOUR CAREER

A job might pay the bills, but a career is something that gives you personal satisfaction while allowing you to achieve financial and lifestyle goals. A career is what you want to do for a living—because you spend a lot of your life working.

When you're making goals for your career, think about:

! What type of work do you really enjoy doing? What do you want to do with your time and energy?

! What are your natural talents and inclinations? Does the career path you're considering take advantage of the things you're good at?

! What rewards do you get from your work? Are you looking for work that gives you extra time? More money? What about work that helps you make a difference in the world?

! What types of opportunity do you have for advancement? Where could you end up in five or ten years on a given career path?

*How long do you want to work? Do you want to work all your life, or are you interested in retiring as early as possible?

*What will you need to know and learn in the career path you're considering? Will you need to further your education? Will you need to learn new skills?

*How will you balance your career and your personal life?

What ideas do you have for goals for your career?

_____

_____

_____

GOALS FOR YOUR FINANCES

Financial goals can include saving for college or retirement, paying off debts, putting away savings for an emergency, owning your own home, or leaving money for your children. You might want to learn how to better manage your money or how to invest. You might want to create a budget and stick to it.

Often financial goals are tied to things that we want. Perhaps you want a new car or a bigger apartment. Maybe you want to reduce your expenses so that you don't have to work as much. Maybe you want to take a vacation to Europe or buy a boat.

Financial goals can require planning and effort, but you can achieve a well-defined financial goal. One of the good things about financial goals is that they're easily measurable. If you want enough money to take a vacation, you can count it in dollars and cents, and you know when you've saved enough. It's also easy to track your progress as your savings continues to grow.

What ideas do you have for goals for your finances?

_____

_____

_____

GOALS FOR YOUR HAPPINESS

The final aim of almost any goal is happiness, but not everything that makes you happy falls into one of the previously discussed areas of your life. There are many things that we do simply because we enjoy them:

! Developing friendships

! Games and puzzles

! Vacations and travel

! Picnics and outings

! Holiday celebrations

! Social events and gatherings

! Discussion groups

What ideas do you have for goals for your happiness?

_____

_____

_____

_____

_____

_____

_____

_____

_____

_____

_____

_____

Goals for Different Types of Results

To create your goal, you need to define the result of your goal. What, exactly, is the goal that you're setting? What do you want to happen, or what do you want to achieve? There are different types of results that you may want to come out of your goal.

ACHIEVEMENTS: WHAT YOU WILL ACCOMPLISH

An achievement can be a state of being (such as becoming a doctor), or it can be an award (such as a degree in English). Achievement goals include a something definite that you plan to accomplish. You could:

! Win a prize or an award

! Earn a degree or a distinction

! Get a specific job

! Get a raise

! Make a certain amount of money

! Finish a project

! Pass a class

! Pass a test

! Organize an event

! Start a non-profit organization

! Start a neighborhood group

Achievement goals are easy to track because you know when you've accomplished them. When you complete your project or earn your degree, you've done what you set out to do.

ACQUISITIONS: WHAT YOU WILL HAVE

An acquisition goal is about getting something that you want. Do you want a new home? Do you want a car? Do you want to buy a wedding ring? Do you want a collection of fine china? Autographs from your favorite sports team? Anything that you can own is an acquisition. You might want:

! To build and decorate a new porch

! To instal solar panels on your roof

! To plant a garden

! To have a dream wedding dress

! To get a food truck for your business

Acquisition goals mean that you will have something to keep at the end of your plan. It's easy to know when you've achieved an acquisition goal because you have your goal—something that you can see and touch.

If you're considering an acquisition goal, make sure you're not choosing something that is too easy. The goal process is not about making a shopping list. A goal is something that requires planning and effort to achieve.

ACTIONS: WHAT YOU WILL DO

An action goal is about doing instead of about completing. Action goals can be the means toward an end... a way to take a step toward your final goal. An action goal could be to take a class or to run a marathon. Notice that these action goals have corresponding goals for achievement. You could have an achievement goal to pass the class or to finish the marathon, or even to win the marathon. The difference is your emphasis. An action goal emphasizes the process. Sometimes it's more important to run in the marathon than to finish it. Sometimes it's more important to take the class than to pass it.

Action goals can help you get started toward accomplishing bigger goals. If you ultimately want to win a marathon, maybe a smaller goal that will get you a step closer is just to run in the marathon. It will give you experience with marathons and give you more confidence to be a better competitor next time.

Action goals get you moving. They're activities, and so they start you moving forward. They don't put you under a lot of pressure, though. That's both good and bad. Pressure can make you work harder. If there's no pressure, what motivation do you have to improve?

At the same time, too much pressure can be self-defeating. If you've never run a marathon before, and your goal is to win, you could easily be overwhelmed. You may not even try. Action goals at least get you started *doing*, and doing is the key to succeeding. That's one reason why action goals make good "starter" goals.

PREVENTIONS: WHAT YOU WILL NOT DO

Many times, our goals are defined by what we do not want. A preventative goal is one that involves not doing something. "I will not smoke." "I will not drink." "I will not eat fast food." "I will not yell at my child."

Preventative goals are negative goals. They describe inaction instead of action. It's important to look for the positive accomplishment that corresponds to the negative preventative goals:

- Negative Goal: "I will not smoke."
  Positive Goal: "I will have healthy lungs."

- Negative Goal: "I will not drink."
  Positive Goal: "I will stay sober."

- Negative Goal: "I will not eat fast food."
  Positive Goal: "I will eat healthy, low-fat meals."

- Negative Goal: "I will not yell at my child."
  Positive Goal: "I will develop a trusting relationship with my child through discussion and conflict resolution."

It's important to recognize negative goals. It can be easy to fall into bad habits that are harmful to ourselves and others. Saying, "I will NOT" can be a strong statement. At the same time, saying, "I WILL" is very important.

BOUNDARIES: WHERE YOU WILL STOP

A boundary goal is similar to a preventative goal, since it's about stopping. Setting a boundary goal, though, is not about stopping something completely. It's about setting a maximum. Think of a boundary goal as a kind of budget.

"I will only spend $100 a week on entertainment expenses."

That's a fairly simple boundary goal. Your boundary for entertainment spending is $100 a week. To accomplish the goal, you'll need to budget. You can budget more than just money. You can budget:

- Time: "I will not watch more than two hours of television a day."

- Energy: "I will not keep lights on in the house more than four hours a day."

- Food: "I will not eat more than one candy bar a week."

- Dry Cleaning: "I will not wear more than one dry-clean outfit a week."

In short, anything that is a resource, anything that you use or do, can be budgeted. Boundary goals set the boundaries for the maximum of a resource that you will use.

MINIMUMS: WHAT YOU WILL DO AT LEAST

A boundary goal is a kind of negative goal. You're limiting or budgeting your resources. You're setting maximums, the most that you will do. Another important type of goal is a minimum goal. A minimum goal sets a minimum that you will accomplish.

Instead of thinking of how you won't spend your time (like watching TV), think about how you will spend your time:

- "I will spend at least two hours a day doing a fun activity with my children."

- "I will spend at least 30 minutes a day exercising."

Instead of thinking of how you won't budget your food (eating candy bars), think about how you will use your food:

- "I will find at least two new, healthy, delicious vegetable dishes to make each week."

❗ "I will eat at least one meat-free dinner a week."

Instead of thinking of how you won't spend your money (on entertainment), think about how you will use your money:

❗ "I will put at least $20 a week into a vacation fund."

❗ "I will donate at least $10 a month to charity."

Turning your limiting boundaries into positive minimums creates an atmosphere of the things you want to do and should be doing, instead of things you don't want to do. You're replacing bad habits with good ideas. Whenever you create budgeting goals, try to include both what you want to limit, like eating junk food, and what you want to encourage yourself to do, like finding delicious ways to eat more vegetables.

My Notes

_____
_____
_____
_____
_____
_____
_____
_____
_____
_____
_____

How to Define a Goal

Once you have decided on a goal in general, you need to make your goal specific. You need to define your goal.

Make Sure Your Goal Is What You Want

Before you begin writing down your goal, make sure that your goal is what you want. Do some brainstorming about what you want out of life, and make sure your goal fits in with your plans. Are you willing to make the commitment to get what you want? Does your goal conflict with anything else that you want? Are you excited about your goal? Are you ready to achieve it?

You probably have some idea of what your main goal is. It might be earning a HSE diploma, going to college, getting a specific job, earning more money, sending your kids to college, or something else. If you're not sure, try using the worksheet at the end of *Plan Smart* to develop a goal. Begin by writing down, in simple terms, what you want. For example, I might start out by writing:

"I want to get a job with the circus."

It's not a well-defined goal yet. It just expresses, simply, what I want after I've thought it through thoroughly.

Write a simple statement of the goal you want to achieve:

_____

_____

_____

Make Sure Your Goal Is about What You Can Do

Is your goal about something that you can control? That doesn't mean that other people and events won't affect your goal. It simply means that you can take responsibility for what you want to achieve.

If my goal stated, "I want to win the lottery," it would be a difficult goal to justify. I can buy a lottery ticket, but that's about all I can do. Winning the lottery is mostly a matter of chance. On the other hand, if I say, "I want to become a doctor," that's a goal I can accomplish. It might be difficult and take a lot of commitment, but it's something that's possible for me to make happen based on my actions.

If I wanted to win the lottery, I could redefine my goal by thinking about what I really want. Instead of winning the lottery, I can redefine my goal to state that I want to make a million dollars. That way, I'm taking control of the end result of my goal.

Remember, a goal is about your own actions and abilities. My goal is to get a job with the circus. That's certainly possible, if I take the right actions. What about your goal?

Is your goal something that you can achieve through your own actions?

_____

_____

_____

If not, redefine your goal to be something you can achieve through your own actions:

_____

_____

_____

Make Your Goal the Right Size

How big is your goal? Is it something that you can accomplish easily? For example, if your goal is to buy a new coat, you might be able to accomplish that by a trip to the store. Your goal isn't really big enough. It doesn't require much effort or planning.

What if your goal is too big? If my goal is to make a million dollars, that might seem overwhelming. Perhaps I need to redefine my goal to say that I want to make $100,000 a year. That's a lot of money, so it's going to be a challenge. On the other hand, the idea of making a million dollars is overwhelming. I might not even know where to start. That doesn't mean you can't have a big goal. You'll have to judge for yourself whether your goal is so big that it'll stop you from even getting started.

My goal is to join the circus. Since I don't have any circus background, it's going to be pretty difficult. Of course, it would be pretty easy if I just wanted to get a job selling tickets or cleaning up after the animals, but that's not really what I want. I'll change my goal to say:

"I want to get a job performing in the circus."

Now, examine your goal to make sure it's the right size.

Is your goal difficult to achieve but possible?

_____

_____

_____

If not, redefine your goal to be something challenging but possible:

_____

_____

_____

Make Your Goal Specific and Measurable

Your goal needs to say exactly what you will do and how you will know when you get there. To make your goal specific, define exactly what you mean. For example, I've got a goal of becoming a circus performer. What kind of performer will I become? I'll need to define the goal better in order to achieve it, because it's going to be a lot different trying to become a sword swallower versus trying to become an acrobat.

To make my goal specific, I'll define exactly what I mean:

"I will get a job as a circus clown."

A specific goal tends to be more measurable. Measurable simply means that you'll know when you get there. You have some way to measure your progress. If your goal is to make $100,000 a year, you can measure your progress in dollars. If your goal is to study a half hour a day, you can measure your progress in time. If your goal is to get a job as a circus clown, you can measure your progress by whether you have a job as a clown. You'll know when you get there.

Now, examine your goal to make it as specific and measurable as possible.

Modify your goal to make it as specific and measurable as possible:

_____

_____

_____

Give Your Goal a Timeline

Your goal needs to include a timeline for when you'll achieve it. Otherwise, how will you know how to structure your plan? How will you know if you're making good progress toward your goal? Giving your goal a timeline also makes it more measurable. As time moves forward, your progress needs to move forward, too.

If my goal is to get a job as a circus clown, I need to take into account how much time I'll need to prepare. I doubt I could get a job next month. I need to learn how to be a clown first, and I need to learn how to get a job as a circus clown. On the other hand, I don't want to make my goal too far away. If I said ten years, I wouldn't have much reason to get started toward my goal right away. Ten years is a long time to become a clown. I'll have plenty of time to get started... tomorrow.

A good timeline isn't too long or too short. It gives you enough incentive to get started toward your goal right away, and it gives you enough time to realistically achieve your goal. I'm going to put a timeline of one year on my goal:

"I will get a job as a circus clown within one year."

Now, examine your goal and give it an achievable timeline.

Modify your goal to give it a timeline that's realistic but not too far in the future:

_____

_____

_____

How Do I Achieve My Goal?

*O*nce you've defined a goal, it's time to get on the road to achieving it. Defining a goal gets you a long way. You've got a specific objective, and you've got a timeline. You know that your goal is achievable, and it's something that you want. Now, all you need to do is take action to get there.

In order to get to your goal, you'll need an action plan. The action plan is a strategy that gives you steps to take so that you can reach your goal.

An action plan is really a part of your goal, and it's the most important part. With a few simple steps, you can build an action plan to achieve your goal.

Building a Hierarchy of Goals

*S*ome of the best goals are big goals. They take a lot of time to achieve, but they can definitely be worth it. How do you make a plan to get to a big goal? The trick is to break your goal down into smaller, more easily achievable pieces.

You need to build a hierarchy of goals. You can develop medium-term goals that build toward your long-term goal and smaller, short-term goals that you can reach right away and which will get you closer to your medium-term goals.

For example, let's take the goal of making $100,000 a year. That's a pretty big goal. How can you get there? It might seem so far away that it's not worth your immediate attention. On the other hand, it's something a lot of people achieve. People get to that goal eventually.

How would you reach that goal? What steps would you take?

Going directly to making $100,000 a year would be nearly impossible. Get-rich-quick schemes just don't work. You need a way to get to your goal that you can achieve, step by step.

You need to plan a path. Breaking up your goal into smaller goals can help you get to your end result.

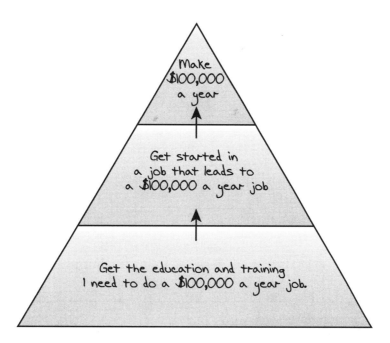

This diagram shows the goals that allow you to build up to your ultimate goal. First, you need to get education and training for a $100,000 a year job. Then, you need to get started in a job that will give you the experience for a $100,000 a year job. That will lead you to your ultimate goal.

The more specific your goal is, the easier it will be to break it up into intermediate goals. The goal of making $100,000 a year isn't really complete, because it lacks a timeline and a specific idea of how you'll make $100,000 a year. Let's say you want to become a doctor making $100,000 a year.

Your short-term goals might be to get a HSE diploma and start going to community college. A medium-range goal might be to get a bachelor's degree in pre-med and get into medical school. All of these goals work together to get you to your ultimate goal.

Take some time to define the intermediate goals that will get you where you want to go.

My ultimate goal:

_____

_____

_____

Medium-range goals that will lead me to my ultimate goal:

_____

_____

_____

_____

_____

Short-range (right now) goals that will lead me to my medium-range goals:

_____

_____

_____

_____

_____

_____

_____

_____

The bigger and more important your ultimate goal is, the more smaller goals you might need to include in your plan. That's okay. A hierarchy of goals gives you easily attainable, short-term goals. You'll know you're making progress, even if the ultimate goal will take time.

Dividing a Goal into Tasks

Creating a hierarchy of goals gives you more goals to tackle, but how do you tackle them? You'll need to prioritize your goals to figure out which short-term goal you're going to work on first. Then, you'll need to divide the goal into tasks.

If your goal is to study at a community college so that you can transfer to a university, you might have a number of tasks.

GOAL: To get transfer credits at a community college for a 4-year university.

TASKS:

1. Register at the community college.

2. Arrange my schedule to take classes and study.

3. Talk to a guidance counselor to plan my classes and to discuss transferring.

4. Register for classes.

5. Buy books.

Your tasks give you a checklist of things to do to get started. Tasks are manageable and give you focus, and they guide you through the process of getting to your goal. Try creating a list of tasks for one of your short-term goals:

GOAL:

_____

_____

TASKS:

_____

_____

_____

_____

_____

_____

_____

_____

_____

_____

_____

_____

_____

_____

_____

Putting Together Your Big Picture Plan

Especially if your ultimate goal is a big one, you'll have a lot of smaller tasks to track. Organize your plan so that you can see your progress and have an overview of the big picture.

Try putting together a goal binder. The first page should have your written, well-defined ultimate goal. On the second page, include a hierarchy of goals that will get you where you want to be.

Then, prioritize those goals. Put each one on a separate sheet, in the order you're going to accomplish them, with a list of tasks that will get you to your goal. As you move through the binder, completing tasks and finishing interim goals, you'll be moving toward your ultimate goal.

How Do I Stay on Track?

Staying on track toward your goal is important. Having a big picture plan broken up into smaller, doable tasks will help a lot. You just have to keep putting one foot in front of the other, and you can get there.

You'll need to stay motivated. That means:

- Remind yourself why you want to achieve the goal.

- Remind yourself what the rewards will be.

- Get friends and family to support you in getting what you want.

- Track your progress.

- Revise your plans as it becomes necessary.

- Remind yourself of how much progress you've made.

- Reward yourself as you make progress.

- Review the progress that you've made and come up with ideas to improve.

- Implement improvements as you keep moving forward.

You'll notice that a big part of motivation is seeing where you are and how much progress you've made. You'll need to know how you're progressing if you're going to reward yourself, come up with ideas to improve, and remind yourself of how much progress you've made. That's why tracking your progress is so important.

How to Track Progress toward Your Goal

How you track your progress toward your goal depends on the results that you want to achieve. Because there are different types of goals, there are different ways to measure your progress. Writing down your progress or representing it visually will help you see how far you've come. It will help you stay motivated.

END-RESULT GOALS

An end-result goal has a final condition—an outcome—something that will mark you reaching your goal. You'll know when you've gotten there, but how do you know how far you're progressing?

There are two ways to measure end-result goals. Some end-result goals have an end result that builds up over time. This is a progressive goal. You're building something bit by bit.

For example, if your goal is to save $5,000 for a dream vacation, you'll save up money over time. That means you'll see the amount of money you have growing.

Here's another example. If your goal is to score in the 90th percentile on a standardized test, you can track your progress with practice tests. Each time your score is higher, you're moving closer toward achieving the 90th percentile score.

If your goal is a progressive goal, you can measure progress with a meter:

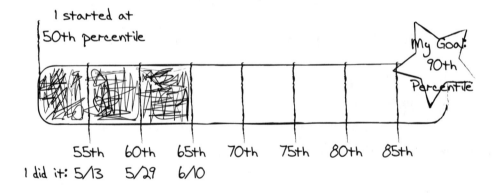

Some end-result goals are not progressive. Instead, you get to your goal through a series of steps. Graduating from college is a step goal. You need to pass a certain group of classes, and then you are awarded your diploma. Each class is a step toward your goal. You can measure the progress toward your goal by the steps you've completed:

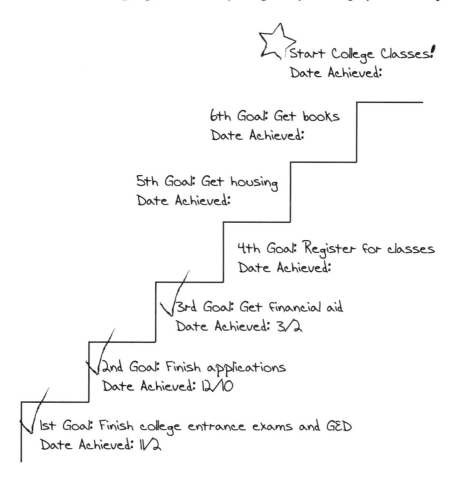

Start College Classes!
Date Achieved:

6th Goal: Get books
Date Achieved:

5th Goal: Get housing
Date Achieved:

4th Goal: Register for classes
Date Achieved:

3rd Goal: Get financial aid
Date Achieved: 3/2

2nd Goal: Finish applications
Date Achieved: 12/10

1st Goal: Finish college entrance exams and GED
Date Achieved: 11/2

CONTINUING GOALS

Many of the goals we've been discussing are continuing goals. They can be difficult to measure because they're ongoing. Achievement goals and acquisition goals are oriented toward a result. There's a specific and measurable end to your goal. Once you've finished it, you can cross it off your list.

It's not so easy to measure the results of other goals. If you have a budgetary goal, how do you measure the results? Let's say that you want to study for at least a half hour a day. That's a minimum goal, and it's about budgeting your time. You can't just measure that you've accomplished it. The goal repeats every day. That means you're measuring your goal on a continuing basis. In fact, your goal is a new goal every day.

The best way to measure a continuing goal is to track your progress over time. You'll need a way to keep tabs on when you meet your goal, when you don't meet your goal, and how far you are from reaching it. As you continue to track your goal, you can see whether you're making progress or backsliding, and you can work to improve.

Here's a sample monthly tracking sheet for studying 30 minutes a day:

Goal: Study 30 minutes each day.

	M	T	W	Th	F	S	Su
Wk 1	:30	:20*	:40	:40	0*	:30	:30
Wk 2	:30	:30	:30	:30	:30	0*	:30
Wk 3	:10*	:10*					
Wk 4							
Wk 5							

What stopped me from studying?

Tu. Week 1: Interrupted by phone call

Fri, Week 1: Had to go to parent-teaching confidence

Sat, Week 2: Too tired

Mon. Week 3: Phone call, Tu. Week 3: Take Johnny to doctor

By putting an asterisk by days the goal wasn't met, the tracker can easily see how she's doing, and by keeping track of what stopped her from studying, she can try to prevent problems. For example, she was interrupted twice by phone calls. Maybe she can make a deal with someone else in the family to answer the phone while she's studying, or she can turn off the phone for a half hour each day.

What to Do When Things Go Wrong

Everyone faces problems and obstacles on the way to their goal. You need to be both flexible and committed to your plan. As you work on each step, you know more. You learn and experience more, so you can update the future steps. You can revise what you need to do to get to your goal, add more steps, and keep track of new developments. You might need to add more intermediary steps or even update your timeline to get to your goal.

Remember, your ultimate goal is the most important thing. How you get there will be, in part, a learning process, full of unexpected bumps in the road. Stay focused on where you're ultimately going and what the rewards are. If you stay committed to your ultimate goal, you can deal with the bumps in the road by being flexible and modifying your plan along the way.

My Notes
_____
_____
_____
_____
_____
_____
_____
_____
_____
_____

Planning for Standardized Tests

You've probably got at least one definite goal: to earn your HSE diploma. That means passing an official test. You can break it out into steps: assessing your needs, studying and preparing, taking practice tests, and finally taking the exam.

Let's walk through setting (and achieving) the goals for your HSE diploma. You can use the study planner at the end of this section to help you plan and achieve your HSE goals.

Define a Timeline

Just as with any other goal, your HSE goal needs a timeline. How soon can you get your HSE diploma? Set a goal. Don't make it impossible, but don't make it too easy, either. If your goal is two years, that's too long! If it's one week, that's probably not enough time! You need a goal that will apply some pressure.

Your goal might be:

> I will pass my HSE exam in the next three months.

Take into account how much studying you need to do and when the test is offered in your area.

Define a Minimum Score

Do you just want to pass? Are you looking for an honors score to get scholarships or get accepted into the perfect college? Set a minimum score that you want to reach in each subject area.

The following chart shows examples of lower-end and higher-end score goals for different HSE tests.

	Low-End Goal to Pass	High-End Goal for Scholarships
HiSET® Exam		
Language Arts—Reading	9	15
Language Arts—Writing	9	15
Essay	2	4
Mathematics	9	15
Social Studies	9	15
Science	9	15
GED® Test		
Reasoning Through Language Arts	150	170
Mathematical Reasoning	150	170
Social Studies	150	170
Science	150	170
TASC Test Assessing Secondary Completion™		
Reading	500	650
Writing	500	650
Essay	2	5
Mathematics	500	650
Social Studies	500	650
Science	500	650

Define a Plan

A good HSE plan starts out with assessment. That's checking up where you're at and what you need to learn to get your HSE diploma. Make your first step to take a practice test or evaluation test.

Then, based on your evaluation, decide what you need to study first. It's best to start with your easiest subjects first. Put the subjects in the order you want to study them.

Now, make a timeline. Make a goal for when you're going to pass each subject, taking into account how much you need to study to be ready.

Implementing the Plan

To implement your study plan, you need to create a new kind of goal: a continuing minimum goal. This is a goal for study time. A good goal would be:

> I will study at least one hour a day, six days a week.

Schedule a time when you're going to study and prepare a space for studying. Make sure your family knows not to interrupt you when you're studying. Another good idea is to get someone to remind you when to start each day.

You'll also need to pull together your study resources. If you have GED Academy™, HiSET® Academy, or TASC Prep Academy, you have everything you need to pass your HSE exam.

Tracking Your Progress

Track your progress every day. Use the Weekly Study Progress Tracker at the end of this section to see how you're doing each week and what you're learning. Thinking about what you've learned at the end of the week will help you remember better and also help keep you motivated to keep learning. You can also think of ways to improve your learning and focus your studying better.

When you think you're ready to take one of the subject-area tests, take another practice test. You'll see how you've improved and how ready you are to meet your goals. You may need to adjust your timeline as you move toward your goals, but that's okay! You'll be able to see that you're making progress, and you'll be surprised how fast you can get to your goal.

My Study Plan

I WILL PASS MY HSE EXAM IN _____ .

Subject	Target Score	1st Practice Test Score	What Order to Study?	2nd Practice Test Score	Ready for Test!

TIMELINE:

Subject	I will be ready to take the test by:	Date took test:	Date passed:

MY STUDY SCHEDULE

I will study _____ hours a day _____ days a week.

Monday: _____ to _____

Tuesday: _____ to _____

Wednesday: _____ to _____

Thursday: _____ to _____

Friday: _____ to _____

Saturday: _____ to _____

Sunday: _____ to _____

Weekly Study Progress Tracker

	SUBJECT STUDIED	**TIME STUDIED**
Monday:	_____	_____
Tuesday:	_____	_____
Wednesday:	_____	_____
Thursday:	_____	_____
Friday:	_____	_____
Saturday:	_____	_____
Sunday:	_____	_____

Reaching Study Time Goals:

How often did I meet my goals for study time?

_____

_____

_____

What prevented me from reaching my goals?

_____

_____

_____

What can I do to reach my goals more often?

_____

_____

_____

_____

Think About Your Studying:

What did I study this week?

_____

_____

_____

_____

How did I improve?

_____

_____

_____

_____

_____

What study techniques did I use?

_____

_____

_____

How can I improve my studying?

_____

_____

_____

_____

_____

Goal Development Worksheet

Use the following questions to think about the goals you want to develop.

What aspects of your life do you want to improve most?

_____

What is your highest priority?

_____

What makes you happy?

_____

Where do you want to be 1 year from now?

_____

Where do you want to be in 5 years?

_____

Where do you want to be in 10 years?

_____

What do you want to change about your life?

_____

What stops you from making that change?

_____

What is something that you've always wanted to do but felt you couldn't?

_____

Why have you felt you couldn't accomplish it?

_____

What do you regret not having done in the past?

_____

What stopped you from accomplishing it?

_____

What types of rewards do you want from life?

_____

What types of goals would provide those rewards?

_____

What do you feel is your biggest personal strength?

_____

How can you best take advantage of that strength?

_____

What do you feel is your biggest personal weakness?

_____

How can you best minimize or accommodate for that weakness?

_____

Monthly Continuing Goal Tracker

Goal: _____

	M	T	W	Th	F	S	Su
Wk 1							
Wk 2							
Wk 3							
Wk 4							
Wk 5							

What stopped me from reaching my goal?

_____

_____

_____

_____

_____

_____

What can I do to reach my goal more often?

_____

_____

_____

_____

_____

_____

_____

Progressive Goal Progress Tracker

Goal: _____

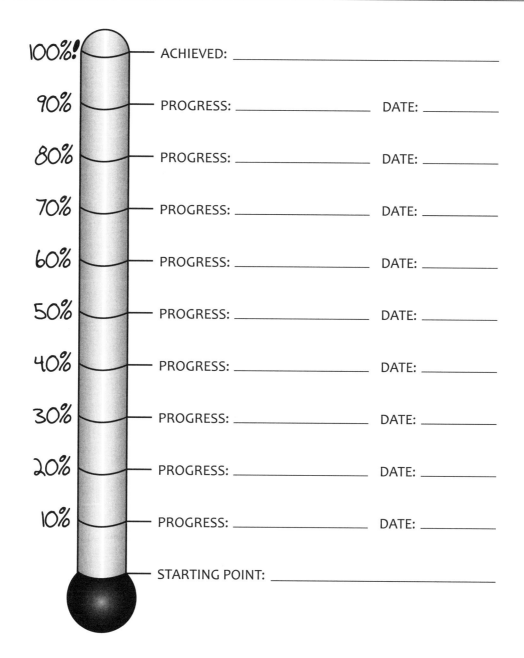

100%! — ACHIEVED: _____

90% — PROGRESS: _____ DATE: _____

80% — PROGRESS: _____ DATE: _____

70% — PROGRESS: _____ DATE: _____

60% — PROGRESS: _____ DATE: _____

50% — PROGRESS: _____ DATE: _____

40% — PROGRESS: _____ DATE: _____

30% — PROGRESS: _____ DATE: _____

20% — PROGRESS: _____ DATE: _____

10% — PROGRESS: _____ DATE: _____

STARTING POINT: _____

Step Goal Progress Tracker

Goal: _____

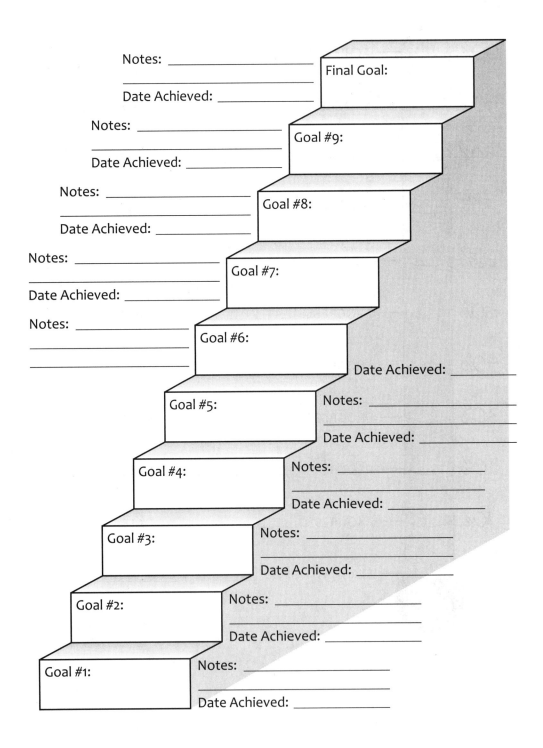

Notes: _____

_____

Date Achieved: _____

Final Goal:

Notes: _____

_____

Date Achieved: _____

Goal #9:

Notes: _____

_____

Date Achieved: _____

Goal #8:

Notes: _____

_____

Date Achieved: _____

Goal #7:

Notes: _____

_____

_____

Goal #6:

Date Achieved: _____

Notes: _____

Date Achieved: _____

Goal #5:

Notes: _____

_____

Date Achieved: _____

Goal #4:

Notes: _____

_____

Date Achieved: _____

Goal #3:

Notes: _____

_____

Date Achieved: _____

Goal #2:

Notes: _____

_____

Date Achieved: _____

Goal #1:

Notes: _____

_____

Date Achieved: _____

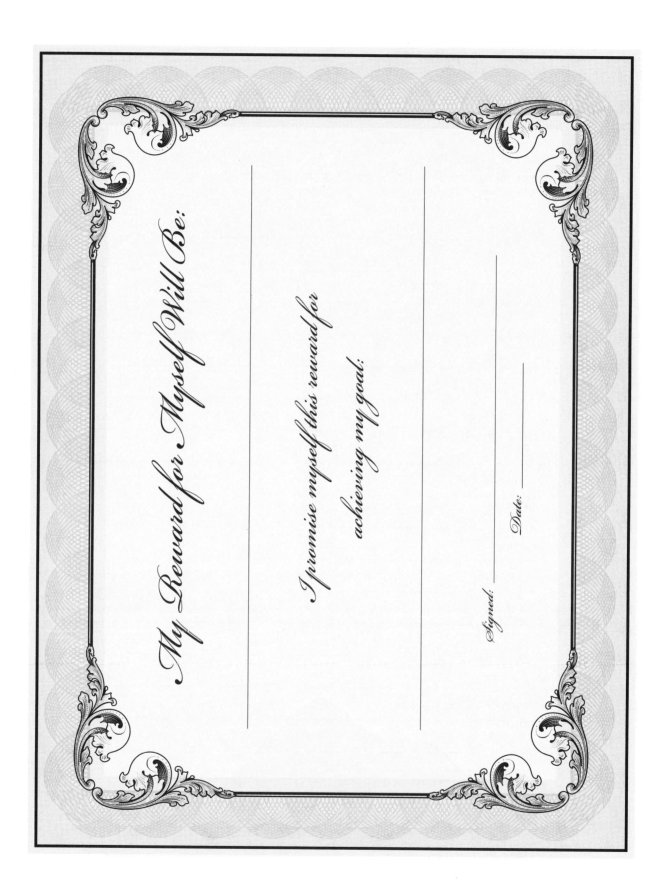

My Reward for Myself Will Be:

I promise myself this reward for achieving my goal:

Signed:

Date:

My Notes

Chapter 3

Learn smart

Secrets to Learning More in Less Time

"Learning is a treasure that will follow its owner everywhere."

—Chinese Proverb

Active Learning

What is learning? Where does it happen? How does it happen? To understand how to learn quickly and easily, start by examining what learning means.

Learning isn't something that happens outside of you or happens to you. It is something that happens in your brain. Learning something new actually changes your brain. You make new connections. You get new information. Just like your body, your brain needs exercise and practice to keep it strong. The more active your brain is every day, the better you'll be at thinking and at learning.

Learning is part of *thinking*. The more you think about something, the more you learn about it.

Learning isn't a *passive* process, where something outside of you makes you know more stuff. Learning is an *active* process. We don't learn by just reading something or listening to someone talk, no matter how interesting they are. We don't learn just by seeing something, either. We get input into our minds from our eyes, our ears, our noses, but to learn, you need to take it a step further. You need to start up the wheels in your mind and get them turning.

It's not hard. It's just a simple step, but it's surprisingly easy to forget to do it! Years of teachers asking you to copy off the board or read a textbook kills the instinct to think about what you're learning. School actually can make people forget how to learn!

Your ability to remember information is dependent on how involved you are with it. The quickest way to learn is for what you're learning to have real meaning for you. That could mean that it's something you're interested in or that it's something that's part of your everyday life.

When you study, your goal is to get as involved in the material as possible. Simply reading a study guide or going to classes and listening to a teacher talk is not going to cut it. How much have you ever learned just sitting in the back of the class? Even good students have days when they learn nothing because they're just sitting and listening instead of being an active learner. Sitting in a classroom is not a learning activity! It gets pretty disappointing results.

How do you activate your learning? How do you get involved with what you're studying? How do you become an active learner?

My Notes

Activating Interest

One great way to become an active learner is to get interested in what you're doing. If something's not interesting, if it's not important to you, how easy is it going to be to take an active role in thinking about it and learning it? Pretty difficult. The worst classes are the boring classes. The worst subjects are the boring subjects.

To learn better, you need to take the "boring" out of learning. The biggest thing high school students complain about is that school is boring! It has very little to do with real life. "When are we ever going to use algebra?" "When am I going to need to know about the French Revolution?" That's what students ask.

The truth is, algebra does have a lot to do with "real life," and so does the French Revolution. They teach us important truths about human nature and the nature of the universe. They teach us how to think better and how to have a bigger understanding of real-life issues. The problem is that out of context, in a classroom, all the connections are removed. You're not learning algebra because you're trying to solve a problem or build something that works. You're learning algebra because *someone else wants you to learn algebra*. It doesn't have meaning to you. It has meaning to someone else.

How do you make learning that *someone else wants you to do* into *learning that is interesting to you*? Can you control your interest? The truth is that you can, but it takes a little bit of effort. Once you activate your interest in what you're learning, you'll learn a lot more—and a lot faster—than you thought you could.

Activate Your Curiosity

One of the things that makes a great learner is curiosity. We're all interested in some things that don't have practical, everyday applications. We go to the zoo to stare at strange animals and comment on how they act, what they look like. We watch TV shows about criminal investigators or doctors or supernatural events. Why? Because we're curious. It's interesting!

Activating your curiosity makes things interesting and makes you a better learner.

We're not naturally curious about everything, though. Some things make us curious, but others don't. In a lot of ways, that defines what our talents are! You can develop your curiosity.

To get more curious:

! Don't just accept what people tell you—and that includes your teacher. Confirm it for yourself.

! Ask, "Why?" Try to figure out how it really works, and why you're supposed to learn it.

! Investigate deeper. Don't just do the minimum... find ways to do more than what's required by a teacher or textbook.

! Look below the surface. Ask, "What would happen if...?" or "Why isn't it like this...?"

! Experiment. Try something new, even if it doesn't seem like it would work.

! Play. Use games and puzzles in your learning. Make goals to challenge yourself, just to see if you can do it.

! Learn to research. Use the Internet, reference books, and the library. You can find out a lot of information on your own.

! Ask more questions. Ask everything that you wonder about, and if you don't have a question, try to find one. If you have a passing question in your mind, don't just ignore it. Look into it. Find out the answer.

! Look for the unusual. In science, look for strange facts. In social studies, look for funny incidents in history. In math, look for math mysteries no one has solved. You can find unusual and interesting tidbits in every subject.

! Don't rush. Stop and smell the roses... or dig into the information a little deeper. Don't be afraid to go off on a side issue. That's part of learning!

What types of things make you curious? Why?

_____

_____

_____

_____

_____

Make Connections to Real Life

Making your study material interesting can be challenging, especially when what you're learning is abstract. It's not something you can relate to. How does it affect the world? How does it affect you? What value does it give you? The more directly you can associate the value of what you're learning with your own life, the easier it will be to become an interested, active learner... and to learn better and faster.

The most common example students talk about is math. Yes, you use addition, subtraction, multiplication, division, and fractions in everyday transactions and keeping track of your finances. Beyond that, there are whole fields of higher math that it's hard to relate to your life. You are taught geometry and algebra as formulas and proofs, but in your everyday life, you never encounter it that way. You may not use all advanced math in your life, but the truth is, a lot of geometry and algebra are useful to you. How can you make the connections?

Here's an example of a math test question. Let's see if we can make a connection to everyday life.

Frank's Frame Shop uses a mathematical formula to figure out the cost of framing photographs. The algebraic formula is:

$$P = 25 + .1xy$$

P is the price of the finished framed picture, and x and y are the lengths in centimeters of the photograph's width and height, respectively. If you took a photograph that was 15 centimeters × 25 centimeters into Frank's shop, how much would it cost to frame it?

1) $34.50

2) $43.75

3) $85.00

4) $25.00

5) $87.50

How do you relate this problem to life? Well, it gives you a little bit of a head start by applying it to picture framing. You at least know what it means to frame a picture. Then it confuses the problem with a complex-looking math formula and information about centimeters—a measurement you probably wouldn't normally use. How do you understand in real-life terms what this problem is talking it about and relate it to what's familiar to you?

The way to do this is to approach the problem from the real-life application, framing the picture. Using an illustration or drawing can often help. Draw a picture of the problem or situation. Write in the measurements and the numbers that represent them. It will help you understand by relating it to something you know, and something you can picture.

Now you've clearly sorted out in your head what letter means what measurement, and it's easier to do the math. Still, that might not be enough. What about trying to find out what the formula actually means? Relate the formula to what you know. Make it make sense, in real-life terms. Okay... so what's the formula actually saying?

$$P = 25 + .1xy$$

"P" is price... and *x* and *y* are the sides of the picture. Remember, this is a price... so all the numbers are dollars. Try expanding the formula to see if it makes sense.

$$P = 25 + .1xy$$

$$\text{Price} = \$25 + \$.1(\text{side 1})(\text{side 2})$$

Is it beginning to come into focus? Let's look further. Multiplying the two sides... that gives you the area of the picture, in square centimeters. You can substitute in "area of the picture in cm²."

$$P = 25 + .1xy$$

Price = \$25 + \$.1(area of the picture in cm^2)

Do you see that point-1 dollar? Put two decimal places on anything that is in dollars to help your understanding. Remember, you can add zeros at the beginning and ending of a number (after the decimal place)—and sometimes that clarifies what it means. The number \$.1 becomes \$0.10—and it makes more sense. In fact, ten cents!

$$P = 25 + .1xy$$

Price = \$25 + (ten cents)(area of the picture in cm^2)

Let's see if we can make this pricing structure make sense...

$$P = 25 + .1xy$$

The price is \$25 plus ten cents per square centimeter of area.

That's saying the same thing... but now it makes sense! Now it relates to something you know about. Dollars and cents. Normal, everyday pricing. You can work with that.

Math isn't the only subject. You can relate all kinds of topics to your own life. Look for connections between your life and whatever you're studying.

❗ History

❊ Research your family tree.

❊ Find out about historic events that your family was involved in.

❊ Visit local historic places.

❊ Find out the history of the town where you live. How does it relate to other historic events happening at the same time?

* What was happening in the world on the day you were born? The day your father or mother was born? Your grandfather or grandmother?

! Civics and Government

* Become involved in local elections.

* Find out how the U.S. Constitution affects Supreme Court decisions made today.

* Find out how your local government works.

* Find out how your tax dollars are spent.

* What laws affect you, personally?

* Read news articles about what's going on in politics today.

! Economics

* What causes the value of your house to increase or decrease?

* What's your credit rating and why? Who's in charge of credit ratings?

* What causes gas and food prices to increase or decrease?

* How does the company you work for determine prices?

* Who are your company's competitors?

! Reading and Writing

* Apply reading techniques that you learn to things you enjoy reading: murder mysteries, romances, science fiction or fantasy books, comic books, magazines, non-fiction books—whatever you enjoy.

* Write about things in your own life.

* Use writing techniques you learn to write letters, memos, a diary, a blog— anything you're interested in or that's valuable to you.

* Keep a reading diary by making a list of all the things you read, even the backs of packages in the supermarket.

✱ Relate book characters' experiences to your own experiences. Try to think of people in your life who are like the characters you read about in some way.

✱ Think about what you already know about a topic before reading about it.

❗ Science

✱ Look in the science news for articles that affect your life.

✱ What do you use in your home that was developed with science? What's the science behind it?

✱ How is your life different now than when you were a child, due to science?

✱ What medicines do you take? How do they work?

✱ How does your body use the foods you eat? What makes food healthy or unhealthy? How is science used in growing food?

✱ What's the science behind cooking and baking?

You can find a lot of connections between the subjects you need to study and your own life.

Strive for Greatness

When you're studying, strive for greatness. Don't be satisfied with "sort of" knowing something. Make your goal to truly understand it. If you're striving for greatness, you're more likely to learn more and actually become interested in the topic you're studying. You can become the expert at what you're studying.

Taking Control of Your Learning

Learn at Your Own Pace

You learn fastest when you control the speed of your learning. This is one of the chief limitations of the classroom. The teacher and the other students control the speed of the learning, but your learning isn't happening with the teacher or with the other students. It's happening with you. It doesn't make sense for someone else to control how quick you go, if the learning's supposed to take place in your head!

Take control of your learning by studying what you need to know when you need it. Control the speed of your learning by:

! Starting with something that's pretty easy for you, instead of starting with something that's really easy or something that's too hard.

! Not moving forward until you've really learned what you're studying.

! Spending as much or as little time as you need on any particular lesson.

! Going back to remind yourself of what you studied before whenever you need to.

Knowing Your Learning Style

How material is presented is important to learning. Some of us are visual learners (seeing), others are auditory learners (hearing), and still others are kinesthetic (moving, touching, doing). Some of us do better when we can see the logic of how the material fits together, while some just want to jump right in with the details. The problem in the classroom is that the material is usually presented in a verbal style, and not all of us assimilate things with just words.

When you study on your own, you have the ability to convert the material to the learning style that works best for you. How do you learn best? Do you want to see what you're learning? Do you want to hear it out loud? Do you need to do something with it for it to make sense and stick in your head?

If you're a visual learner, you can translate the concepts into pictures. Draw what you're trying to learn. Make it into a diagram or another visual. Try to remember things by associating them with pictures. Find videos of what you're learning.

If you an auditory learner, try reading out loud when you have to read. Get a tape recorder to record yourself and play it back. Find audio information on the Internet, including video blogs and podcasts. Try translating your learning into music!

If you're a kinesthetic learner, try finding interactive learning games to play. Try doing experiments for science or doing puzzles. Try interactive online programs that allow you to play with concepts in geometry. Even use cotton swabs, toothpicks, play blocks or dough, or other everyday objects to visualize what you're learning. Go out and meet people and visit places.

Turning your learning into stories or even dances can help almost any kind of learner. Be creative about where your learning takes you! You will learn most effectively when you can access the material in a style that best fits your personal learning style.

Keeping Track of Progress and Getting Feedback on Your Learning

Getting feedback as you learn is essential. The more immediate and meaningful the feedback is, the quicker we learn. If we have to wait days or weeks until the papers and tests are corrected, we lose the opportunity to connect our learning efforts with the outcome. The best learning situation gives you immediate feedback on your progress.

Feedback is a critical part of the learning process, one that's often overlooked. The more immediate and meaningful the feedback is, the quicker people learn.

Consider how many classroom situations work: Information is presented over days or weeks—or sometimes over months. Then students are tested. Until they see test results, students may not know whether their learning is effective.

A good study program should include continuous opportunities and methods for you to connect your learning efforts with your results. This way, you can quickly identify whether you've learned the material and what you need to learn better. It reinforces your learning by using information quickly and frequently. By using information, you learn it faster.

Taking tests and quizzes is one way to get feedback, but it isn't the only way. Consider these strategies:

! Discuss knowledge and information you learned or studied—and don't limit yourself to study or classroom times. At lunch or dinner, tell your family what you've read, studied, or learned. Talk to friends, coworkers, and classmates about what you learned. This can also help you make connections to your life and find interesting things about what you're learning.

! Try to explain what you learned to someone else. This is a good way to get your children involved in your studying. You can also take turns with a study partner. See if you can teach what you've learned. Teaching can sometimes help us learn even better!

! Once you learn material and gain new knowledge, use it. Use it every chance you get. Using new knowledge ensures ownership and understanding, and it enhances critical-thinking skills. Using your knowledge and new skills will also build your confidence and reduce test stress.

Understanding How You Remember

Memory is like learning. It's an active process. It does not happen by just listening to someone talk or just reading the material. Things are imprinted onto our memory when we create multiple connections within the brain. Without multiple paths to the idea or fact, we have difficulty retrieving it. You know the feeling of a memory that's there, but not quite accessible—the sensation like something's just on the tip of your tongue. Your brain is rapidly searching the millions of pathways to find the connection to the information you need. Increasing the number of connections is what improves our memory process.

When people say they have a "bad memory," or they can't seem to remember anything, what they are really saying is they have not learned how to memorize effectively. Here are some ways to improve your memory.

1. Always over-learn the material. Don't quit reviewing and testing yourself until you can do it backwards and forwards. We have a tendency to stop the memorization process as soon as we see that we have been able to retrieve the material once. Don't stop there. Keep practicing and reviewing and testing yourself until it comes almost unconsciously. This not only builds your confidence with the material but imprints it better in your long-term memory.

2. Time is a big factor in memorization. If you attempt to learn something too quickly, it imprints only your short-term memory. If you stretch the learning cycle out over a long period of time, then you increase the chance for it to be imprinted on your long-term memory. Consequently, it is better to practice and review material over many days or weeks than to try to cram the learning into a short period of time, like a day or two. Take long breaks between reviews of the material. You will find that each time you practice and review you lose less and less of the material.

   What makes your memory even stronger is testing it over time. Let your brain know that this isn't just information you need right now. It's information you'll want to recall later.

   * Study the information until you can recall what you need and then stop.

   * Fifteen minutes later, try to remember it. Really struggle to recall. If you can't, study it again and try again in fifteen minutes.

✱ An hour later, try to remember it. Really struggle to recall. If you can't, study it again and try again in an hour.

✱ The next day, try to remember it. Really struggle to recall. If you can't, study it again and try again the next day.

✱ At the end of a week, try again! Your brain should know by now that this is material you'll need to recall after some time has passed, and your connections to it should be strong.

3. Help yourself to remember with retrieval clues. Creating multiple pathways to the material can be facilitated by clues that jog your memory. You can help yourself remember by remembering related items you studied at the same time. For example, you can jog your memory on how to solve an algebraic formula by remembering the specific problem you studied and how you solved it in your practice. You can remember the shape of the formula or make a picture out of it. You can make a rhyme or song about the formula. You can think of related problems and the step-by-step process you used to solve them.

Another way to help yourself retrieve the material is to visualize the day you worked on the material and recreate the process you went through that day. Recreate as much about the day as you can. What were you wearing, what did you eat, what time of day did you study, where you were you sitting and so on? Picture the notes you made and visualize writing them down. Remember the mistakes you made while you were learning the material and what you did to correct them. The more detail you can recreate, the more pathways you will open to the material you are trying to remember.

4. Organize the material into chunks and relate the chunks to each other in memorable ways. For example, when you study geometry, organize the material into pictures of the geometric objects. Put all the material about circular shapes together and then sort that material again into two-dimensional shapes about area and three-dimensional shapes about volume. Relate the shapes to common objects you are familiar with while you are solving the problems. For example, relate a cylindrical volume problem to common household objects like a glass or jar or a rectangular volume problem to the bed in a pick-up truck. Practice with these objects to make the math familiar and real.

5. Sleep has been found to greatly improve memory. Studies have shown that you are more likely to remember things you study right before you go to sleep. Review lists, math formulas, and vocabulary words before you go to bed, and you will find you remember more the next day.

6. Use mnemonic devices to improve your memory. A mnemonic device is anything that helps jog your memory. It can be rhymes, organizational methods, numbering systems, cue cards, writing the material down, alliterative phrases, associations, acronyms, cram sheets, and visualizations. The idea is to connect the material to be remembered with something else that is easier to remember.

Rhymes, acronyms, and alliterative phrases work very well. Advertisers and marketers use mnemonic devices all the time to help you remember products or services. Try your own mnemonics! For example, to remember how to solve word problems, you might make up an acronym to help you remember the four-step solution method: Q-C-M-C

? **Question:** What is it asking?

? **Clues:** What information do I need to solve it?

? **Method:** How am I going to solve it?

? **Check:** Does the answer make sense?

You could relate the four-step process to something you already know how to do, like playing video games. Use mnemonic devices as much as you can. Taking time to make things easy to remember can save you hours of study.

Studying a Text for Understanding

A lot of our studying comes from reading. We read textbooks, stories, online articles, magazines, and newspapers. There are a lot of other types of visual, audio, and kinesthetic materials out there, but the truth is, you still need to read to get the information you need.

Studying is more than reading. You don't want the information to go into your brain and then just leave. Just like any kind of learning, studying a text needs to be active learning. There are some simple ways that you can read more effectively and learn faster and easier. Try different techniques and strategies and find out which ones work best for you.

Navigating Your Reading

When you're reading, it's important to be able to navigate. You don't have to read a textbook in order. The point is to find the information that you need. You personalize your reading by navigating to what you want to know. Titles, indexes, glossaries, pictures, bold words, capitalized words, and charts and graphs all give you information about what's in the text and help you find information that you need.

There are other clues to tell you what's in the text and help you read faster and learn better. If you're reading a twenty-page chapter with no pictures and all text, how do you find the main ideas and sort out what the writer is trying to say? The words on the page are still organized into paragraphs, and because the writing is *organized*, you can find what you need by understanding that organization.

One trick in reading paragraphs is to look at the first sentence and the last sentence for important information. The same is true of sections of a book. The first paragraph in a section and the last paragraph will have important ideas and summaries of the other information. Always pay attention to the first and the last.

There are even more clues that you'll find in writing. Different information is organized in different ways.

! **Look for lists.** A list of steps might tell you how to do something. A list of important points gives you main ideas.

❗ **Look for comparisons.** Sometimes writers compare and contrast two or three ideas. If the information you're reading is a comparison, it's easiest to understand it by organizing it as a comparison—as a table or a Venn diagram.

❗ **Look for timelines.** Some writing is like a story. It tells what happened over time, from beginning to end. You can remember the events in sequence. Sometimes the story is a long one, over many years, and you might even find a literal timeline in what you're reading.

❗ **Look for definitions and descriptions.** Both definitions and descriptions tell you about something. What is it, exactly? Definitions and descriptions mark important concepts in what you're reading.

❗ **Look for cause and effect.** Some writing shows the connections between causes and their results. Look for cause-and-effect relationships in what you're reading.

All of these types of information give you ways to organize ideas, and organizing ideas is the key to remembering them and understanding them. Your mind absorbs patterns much easier than random facts, so identifying these patterns will help you make sense of what you're reading.

Taking Notes

Whether you are attending classes or doing home study, it is critical that you take notes and then organize those notes in a way that maximizes your learning. Note taking is important for several reasons. First, it forces you to think about the material beyond just hearing or reading it. The more you can think about it the better you learn it. Secondly, note taking requires organizing the material, and if that organization is done in a logical way, then you are already one step closer to organizing it in your mind.

Note taking is not always easy, especially in the classroom. It requires that you split your attention between what the teacher is saying (or what you're reading) and writing the main points down on paper. Often a teacher will write the key information down on the board. Then, you can copy it. Will you know why it's important later, though? In a lot of cases, it's better to write down what you're getting out of the lecture, not just what the teacher is writing on the board. When you're reading, you won't have a teacher telling you what your notes should be. In a way, that's helpful. When you're taking notes, you're being active by:

! Choosing what **you** think is important

! Restating what you read or heard in **your** own words

! Connecting what you read or heard to what **you** already know

! Putting your notes in an order **you** think makes sense

The most important step in note taking, whether it is for a classroom or for home study, is the review and reorganization of your notes. To get the most of your notes:

! Review your notes after you read or after class. Organize them in an order that makes sense to you, noting connections between ideas or between important points.

! Review all your notes once a week. Make sure the notes make sense to you. If it doesn't make sense, rewrite it so it does. Put together key ideas and add information that seems to be missing.

The review has several benefits. First, it refreshes your mind with the material. Second, it gives you the opportunity to identify the things you need to know. Third, it helps you organize the material, and that helps you learn faster and remember better.

While you're reviewing your notes, choose methods of organization that will help you best study the material. Different techniques will be helpful for different materials. Try some of these suggestions:

! Make lists of key words so that you can memorize them.

! Make a numbered list of steps to remember a process.

! Make an outline of the information so that you see the relationship of ideas and facts to each other.

! Make a diagram or web showing how different ideas relate to each other.

! Put facts or ideas in a table.

! Organize the information in a pyramid to show a hierarchy of ideas.

! Compare and contrast ideas in a Venn diagram.

Note taking can seem like an extra step in the learning process. Remember the first principle of learning: involvement. Note taking forces you to get more involved with the material. Yes, it can be tedious, but it is often the difference between learning and not learning, or between a lot of studying and just a little.

My Notes

NOTE-TAKING SYSTEM: CORNELL NOTES

The Cornell system is a way to take notes during a lecture, but you can also adapt it to taking notes during reading. The Cornell system uses a note-taking page that's divided up into sections. Your main notes will be divided into two columns. The column on the left will be about a third of the page, and the column on the right will be about two-thirds of the page.

On the smaller side, jot down headings, keywords, main ideas, summaries, and important points to remember.	On the larger side, take down all the details that explain the summaries or important points. Be as complete as you can, so you have all the information.

Summarize at the bottom of the page in a box that goes across both columns.

The Cornell system has 5 R's for taking notes: Record, Reduce, Recite, Reflect, Review.

1. **Record:** Record as much as possible on the right-hand side of the page. Don't write word-for-word, but get all the details in a complete summary. You'll need to understand your notes later, remember, so you'll want to be clear and complete. This column is where you'll do most of your note-taking during class or during reading.

2. **Reduce:** Use the left-hand column to write cues or keywords that will tell you what the big ideas are. Make these as short as possible. You're distilling ideas into big main concepts, as well as creating organization and easy-to-remember groupings. Also, make your summary at the bottom of the page. This will help you distill all the ideas into a main, overall idea.

3. **Recite:** Study your notes by covering up the right-hand column. Look at the keywords and phrases in the left-hand column and try to remember all the details. Restate to yourself the whole lecture or reading as carefully and completely as possible based on the keywords that you've chosen. Those keywords will stimulate your memory!

4. **Reflect:** Ask yourself what the ideas you're studying mean. How do they fit into the world? Why are they important? Can you apply them to your life? Do they open up more questions for you? Are they useful? Do they generate any new ideas about the world for you?

5. **Review:** Review your notes every week to learn better!

CORNELL NOTES TEMPLATE

What I'm Studying: _____

Keywords and Cues	Detailed Notes

Summary

Reading Strategy: KWL

A great way to get more out of what you're reading is a reading strategy called KWL. That stands for Know, Want-to-Know, Learned. This reading strategy helps you relate what you're reading to your life so you learn more and understand better. You can also adapt the strategy to listening to a teacher in the classroom.

1. **KNOW…Ask Yourself, What Do I Already Know?** The first thing to do is look at the topic you're studying. Before going to class or reading, take some time to think about what you're going to study. What do you already know about it? What can you tell by looking at what you're reading? Are there pictures? What's the title? What's the subject? Does it remind you of anything? Write down what you already know.

2. **WANT TO KNOW…Ask Yourself, What Do I Want to Know?** The second thing to do is think about what you want to know from reading or from your class. What do you think you'll learn? What would be interesting to know? Write down what you want to know and any questions that you have.

3. **LEARNED…After Reading, Ask Yourself, What Did I Learn?** It helps you remember things to think about them after reading them. After reading (or after going to class), what did you find out about the topic? Did you find the answers to your questions? Did you learn anything else, anything new? Write down what you learned. Do you have any unanswered questions? Try to find out the answers for yourself!

Use the following simple worksheet for the KWL method.

KWL WORKSHEET

What I'm Studying: _____

Know	Want to Know	Learned

Reading Strategy: Restating and Summarizing

It's easy to think that to read something, you'd just read it. However, to remember something you read, you have to do something to fix it in your mind so you don't forget. Otherwise, you can study and study and then not remember anything you've read, or you can read something and not really understand it. It's just words, with no meaning.

Restating and summarizing are two strategies to remember what you read and to make sure you understood it.

Restating means that you say something again in your own words. This is a good technique to help you understand and remember something that's short. You can restate a sentence or a paragraph that you've read.

Summarizing means that you write or state the most important information about what you read. It's like you're writing down the main ideas of what you read. Maybe you write a paragraph saying what the main points of a whole article are. This is good for longer readings and to help you figure out what the main ideas are.

The difference between restating and summarizing is that you don't leave anything out when you restate. You just say it again in your own words. In summarizing, you only give the most important points, in your own words.

Reading Strategy: SQ4R

SQ4R is a reading strategy that's very helpful in reading textbooks and other study material. SQ4R stands for "Survey, Question, Read, Respond, Review, Reflect." Here's what you do:

1. **Survey:** Don't start reading right away! Instead, look at the page. What are the titles? Headings? Bold words? Pictures? Captions? Graphs? Look at the big things on the page and try to understand the main idea or topic.

2. **Question:** Don't start reading yet! Based on what you looked at in your survey, ask some questions. What do you want to know? If it's your book, write questions on the page, next to the title and pictures. You can also write on a piece of paper. Ask as many questions as you can imagine.

3. **Read:** Now it's time to read! If it's your book, underline things, circle new words, and write down ideas while you read. If it's not your book, write notes on a piece of paper. This is active reading… you're thinking while you're reading!

4. **Respond:** While you're reading, you want to find the answers to your questions, too. You either have your questions written on the page or on a separate paper. Now, write the answers that you found by the questions.

5. **Review:** After you're done reading, look back at what you did. Look over the pages you read. Did you find all the answers to your questions? Did you miss anything? Do you understand what you read? Do you have some new questions?

6. **Reflect:** Put what you read away. Now, stop and think about it. Talk about it with a friend or write a diary entry about what you think. Do you agree with what was said? Did you find something interesting or new? Did you learn something? Are you still confused about anything?

SQ4R is a way to help you be an active learner. You're not just reading. You're thinking, making connections, and organizing ideas. You're asking questions and getting answers. That's a better way to learn.

Put What You Read to Work

Don't let your reading stay in the book. Put it to work by answering questions, doing activities, and making learning an interactive experience. Use what you study in your everyday life as much as possible. You'll learn faster because it has real meaning to you!

Creating a Learning Environment

It's important to make time to study, but it's also important to have a good space where you can study. Why? Because you need to be comfortable and have as few distractions as possible to concentrate on studying. How can you study if you're hungry or if your chair is uncomfortable or if your friends are IM'ing you in chat all the time?

Finding the Right Study Space

Here are 10 tips for a great study space.

1. Choose a space that's comfortable. Make sure your chair and desk are comfortable to sit and work at and make sure your desk gives you enough workspace. Do you need some space to get up and stretch? Make sure you have it. Don't give yourself an excuse to leave your study space.

2. Choose a space where you feel at home. Feel free to decorate your study place with motivational pictures or posters. Keep some items there (photos, notes to yourself, notes from your family) to remind yourself of your goal, and congratulate yourself on what you've accomplished so far.

3. Choose a space that is quiet or where you control the sound. Most people study best in a quiet area, either with no noise or with quiet music in the background. You might need more noise, or no noise, or even white noise, like the TV turned to an empty channel. Find out what works for you, but make sure you can control the level of noise in your study space. You might want to choose a study time when there isn't a lot of noise.

4. Choose a space that is distraction-free. Don't keep toys or games at your desk, and turn off any Internet messaging software or other computer programs that might distract you.

5. Choose a space where you can be alone. You might make a sign: "No interruptions please! Studying!" Leave your cell phone in the other room… and turn off the ringer.

6. Choose a space that's always accessible. You can't study if someone else is on the phone in your workspace or getting a snack at your desk. Your workspace should be your space… someplace that's always open to you when you need it. If you schedule regular study time every day, you can make sure that your study space is off limits to everyone else during that time.

7. Choose a space with everything that you need. Your study area should have a computer, your study materials, a study plan for you to track your progress, paper, pencils, pens, a dictionary, a calculator… anything you need for your studying.

8. Choose a space where you can be organized. Keep your materials where you can get at them easily but where they don't make a lot of clutter. You might want to go to an office supply store and buy some inexpensive organizers where you can keep your materials.

9. Choose a space that's well-lit. Make sure you have a lamp at your desk or good light coming in from a window. A well-lit area will keep you awake and able to focus, and it will cut down on eyestrain, especially if you're reading.

10. Choose a space that's just the right temperature. If you're uncomfortable, you can't concentrate on studying. If you're too hot or too cold, you're making it harder to learn. If you need a space heater in the winter or a fan in the summer, make sure that you've got one in your study space.

Make your study space comfortable and inviting. It will help you keep to your study schedule, and it will help you study more effectively and learn more quickly.

Practicing Learning

Learning is something that requires practice. Try applying different learning skills and techniques to what you're studying, as well as to your everyday life. You'll find that with practice, your learning skills become second nature. Instead of merely passively reading or listening, you're actively taking in and applying knowledge. All your skills will improve faster and easier once you're a practiced learner.

Here is a good example of how one successful student gained real knowledge through the application of learning skills:

Learning Case Study: Maria's Story

Maria, studying for a reading test, encountered an unfamiliar word in a literary passage, the word "superfluous." Not an easy word.

At first, the word just seemed confusing to Maria. She wanted to check the word in a dictionary but remembered that she wouldn't be able to use a dictionary at test time. She had learned in her online class how to look for context clues to find word meanings, especially if the word seemed to be important to the reading. She found three words that seemed to point back to the word "superfluous." They were "extra," "over-abundant," and "excessive." Maria was fairly sure that all the other words meant a large amount, maybe even "too much." She also analyzed the word superfluous, and identified "super" at the beginning of the word. That made her certain that she was right—the word superfluous obviously meant something extra. Then, her dictionary confirmed it.

Through the next few weeks, Maria began using new words she was learning during conversations as well as trying to figure out words while she was reading, even if she wasn't studying. At first it was hard. Using new words seemed unnatural, and she had to really think about them. After a short time, though, new words came to her more naturally. She developed complete ownership of her new knowledge. Not only was her vocabulary expanding, but she discovered that it became easier to move through reading that she needed to do for studying. Her feedback scores were climbing. Also, writing essays seemed much less challenging. Not only were her reading and analysis skills improving, but her writing skills reflected her work.

Maria was pleased at her new ability and started really enjoying her studies. Studying now seemed more of a hobby instead of a chore. She wasn't the only one impressed. Her boss asked her to lead a training program since she was demonstrating quick abilities to understand, analyze, and explain new information.

Maria's story is an excellent example of all three principles that speak to reinforcement of the learning process.

When Maria first encountered a difficulty, she controlled the speed of her learning. She slowed the pace of her learning and really spent some time thinking about the information. She took an active role in the learning process. Maria confirmed her learning through the dictionary, giving herself some feedback.

Then, Maria used her new knowledge, giving herself more feedback, not only on one word but on the *method* she was using to learn. She found that she could use that method to learn a lot more. By using it in everyday situations, at work and in conversations, she quickly became the rightful owner of the knowledge. She became the expert, and all her skills began to improve because of it.

This new knowledge benefited Maria at work as well as in her studying. Her knowledge was reflected in her test scores, improved her critical-thinking skills, and created an enthusiastic attitude good for learning and a terrific career opportunity.

Learning toward a Goal

To make your learning meaningful, you should always be learning toward a goal. That doesn't just include your ultimate goal: getting your diploma, certificate, or degree, or passing a class. You need to have a goal each time you sit down to learn.

When you read a passage, ask a question about it. When you approach a math formula, make it your goal to understand what the formula means and why it's used. When you approach a social studies reading, try to understand how it affects the government and laws today. Make a goal out of every learning activity.

My Notes

Reflecting on Your Learning

After you've studied or read or gone to class, you're not done learning. A lot of learning is done by reflection. That means thinking about what you've learned, how you've learned it, how successful your learning is, and how you can improve your learning. Reflecting is expanding and continuing your thinking. It keeps your brain active and involved. After all, that's the key to learning. Use these questions to reflect on your learning.

What have I learned?

_____

_____

How have I progressed toward my overall learning goal?

_____

_____

What study and learning techniques did I use?

_____

_____

Did the study and learning techniques I used help me? How?

_____

_____

How can I improve the learning or study techniques that I used?

_____

_____

Do I have notes or records that I can study later?

_____

_____

Did I delve deeper into the issue to understand it better? How?

_____

_____

What was interesting about what I studied?

_____

_____

_____

What was boring about what I studied? Can I make it more interesting?

_____

_____

_____

What elements of what I studied were visual (seen)? Auditory (heard)? Kinesthetic (moving, doing)?

_____

_____

_____

How can I use what I've learned in my life?

_____

_____

What was easiest for me to learn? Why?

_____

_____

What was hardest for me to learn? Why?

_____

_____

Do I need help to understand what I need to know? Where can I go for help?

_____

_____

_____

How can I investigate deeper into what I'm learning?

_____

_____

_____

How can I do something creative with what I'm learning?

_____

_____

_____

What should I study next?

_____

_____

Chapter 4

Feel smart

How to Motivate Yourself and Eliminate Anxiety

"Keep away from those who try to belittle your ambitions. Small people always do that, but the really great make you believe that you too can become great."

—Mark Twain

Feeling Smart

"I've tried to get my HSE diploma, and I've failed."

"I bought a study program, but I never used it."

"I went to classes, but I dropped out. It's too much."

"I just can't keep going."

"It's no use, I'll never get my diploma."

Do any of these common thoughts sound familiar? Probably! One of the biggest obstacles to getting your HSE diploma can be your own attitude. Anxiety, fear, and lack of motivation are huge problems, and they're the hardest ones to overcome. It's not easy to fight your own feelings. How do you learn to feel better about yourself? How do you learn to be confident?

Because the truth is, you can be successful and accomplish your goals, no matter what teachers or family members have told you in the past. Negative voices from the past, fear of failure, and stress are all very real, but they're problems that you can overcome.

Visualizing Your Goal

Making It Real, Believing It's Possible

A lot of the time, the goal you want seems impossible. It doesn't feel achievable. It's something you've never done before, and it can seem pretty far away. Making your goal seem real and possible and doable is a key to actually achieving it. If you believe you can, you'll be motivated to do it.

Here are some suggestions to help you make your goal seem achievable.

- Write down your goal and what you'll do when you achieve it. Writing something down makes it more real and concrete.

- Outline the steps you'll take to get to your goal. Small steps are much easier to see as achievable than big goals, so this isn't just about planning. It's about motivation.

- Write down the reasons you're trying to achieve your goal, the people you're doing it for, and the rewards you hope to gain. Look at them to remind yourself why you're doing this and to keep up your motivation.

- Write down the qualities you possess that will help you achieve this goal.

- Give yourself affirmations. Tell yourself "I will..." and "I can..."

- When you reach an obstacle, confront it. Make a plan to overcome it. Don't let it overwhelm you. Once you sit down and think through how you can get over the obstacle, it won't seem as big or as hard.

- Take a few moments each day to sit down in a quiet place, close your eyes, and picture yourself achieving your goal. See as many details as possible. Visualize the path you'll take to get there, and what you'll do once you arrive.

- Talk to your family and friends about your goals. Commit to them. Make sure everyone knows what you're doing. It'll help prevent you from backing out, and talking about goals to others helps you make them real. It helps make them more achievable.

- Take a first step. This isn't just something you're dreaming about doing. It's something you're actually doing.

! Put a picture that symbolizes your goal somewhere prominent—on the refrigerator, at your desk. This will remind you what you're working toward.

! Expect that you'll reach a day when you just don't want to sit down and study. Know what your excuses are: that you're too busy, that it's too hard, that you're too tired. Be prepared to combat them before you get there. What will you do to force yourself to overcome your inner stumbling block?

! Be aware when you start having negative thoughts, like that you can't do it or that it's too hard, or that failure is coming. Get rid of those thoughts quickly. Just let go of them if you can, or find a positive thought for every negative one. Get a friend to tell you why your negative thoughts are wrong, or just think about them realistically. Are these thoughts helpful? Are they real? Can you think of evidence to show they're not true? Most likely, your negative thoughts just random feelings that don't mean anything! It's natural to be insecure of have self-doubt. Let it go! You don't need to listen to it.

! If you fall off the horse and miss a day of studying, don't let it become an excuse to stop. Get right back on the next day and don't look back.

! Plan time to relax and de-stress. Before or after a study session, take a few moments just to breath deeply and enjoy a moment of quiet. Take one day off a week from your study schedule. Make sure you have time to exercise or take a bath. Relieving stress on a regular basis will prevent a break-down under pressure.

Creating a Supportive Environment

You shouldn't expect to do it all yourself. You can't take on a big task without help. Don't underestimate what your family and friends can do to help you. The negative voices from childhood, from school, or from work experiences can be very damaging. It's important to create positive, supporting voices to help you achieve your goals. That means establishing a community to help you, and how you create a supportive learning environment will depend on your situation.

Your Family

Your family can be great motivators and supporters. If your family is unhappy or negative about what you're doing, it can cause significant problems in your progress. On the other hand, if your family is supportive, they can help you move forward quickly and easily and feel good about what you're doing. The following steps will help you create a supportive environment in your family:

1. **Talk to your family.** Sit down and explain why this is important to you and what you hope to accomplish. Explain why it's difficult but also why it's worthwhile. Tell them that you're doing it for them as well as for yourself and that you expect their help and support. Even young children can understand that this is important for you (and if learning's important to you, it's more likely to be important to them). Talk about any problems or issues your family has with what you're doing. If you can't get them to support you, at least get them to agree to not interfere.

2. **Set up ground rules.** Your family can interfere with your study time and space, so you'll need to set up ground rules to make sure you have the time you need. Explain what your schedule will be and get your family to help give you the quiet time you'll need to study.

3. **Get support.** Most of the time, your family can help you. They want you to succeed! You might even find that some members of your family can help study with you. Maybe your family can write you motivational letters and notes. Maybe they can arrange rewards when you reach milestones in your journey toward your goal. They can help remind you when it's time to study and make sure you keep with your work.

Your Friends

Your friends can help you out in much the same way as your family. Explain what you're doing. Tell them what kind of support would be most helpful. Do you need someone to stay on your case to make sure you keep up with studying? Do you need someone to take you out for drinks when you pass a test? Do you need someone to babysit the kids for an hour each night or to give you a call to remind you to start studying? Don't keep your friends in the dark. Make them part of your supportive community. Give them an opportunity to help.

Online Communities

Online communities can be a great resource for motivation and support. Start your own blog or page about your progress and what you're doing. Family and friends can keep in touch and leave comments, and you may even meet other people doing the same thing. Ask questions in online forums. Join online groups. Start your own online group! Read other people's experiences and share your own.

Classmates, Teachers, and Community Groups

If you're enrolled in classes, your classmates can be an invaluable resource. Studying in a group can be more effective than studying on your own because it gives you immediate support. You're in a learning community. Get a study group together or find a study partner in your class.

Your teachers are also a resource. Don't be afraid to ask for help if you don't understand something. The more you ask and communicate, the more you'll learn—and the better you'll feel about yourself.

Are there adult learning centers in your community? Even if you're not enrolled in classes, try posting ads for study partners or a study support group in your community. You might find there are other people striving for the same goals who can help you. Try local bulletin boards and online local centers.

Rewarding Yourself for Success

A simple motivator is rewarding yourself when you're successful. Don't be afraid to cheer yourself on and to get others involved in the celebration. If you've worked hard and accomplished something, you deserve to celebrate. Make sure the treat is something you'll really enjoy. Examples of rewards could be:

! Take time out for yourself. Enjoy a ball game or a spa day.

! Go out with your friends or family.

! Buy yourself something that you want. Make your rewards bigger and bigger as you move forward.

! Treat yourself to a dinner you enjoy but can't have all the time.

! Have a date night with your spouse.

! Have a party.

! Have a "you've done it" cake.

! Anything you'll enjoy!

Don't just save up your rewards for when you accomplish your ultimate goal. The key is to set smaller, intermediate goals as you work. You don't become successful overnight. You become more and more successful as you go along. Each milestone, each marker on your journey is its own success. Reward yourself.

Setting Up Motivational Reminders

Motivation isn't something that you do just once. It's something that you have to do on an ongoing basis. Make it part of your regular routine.

- Have family members leave you motivational notes.

- Have a friend send you a daily motivational text message.

- Have a friend call you each day to see how you're doing toward your goal.

- Keep a book of motivational sayings and read one each day.

- Give yourself a small reward every day for doing your work.

- Get a motivational desktop daily calendar.

- Use a motivational picture as your computer desktop background or screensaver.

- Keep a journal or blog to keep track of your progress and keep yourself motivated.

- Bookmark some motivational websites and visit them every day.

- Every day, tell your family and friends what you've done toward your goal that day.

How to Eliminate Test Anxiety

If the number one fear is public speaking, then the number two fear among students is probably test taking. Taking tests, trying new things, striving to succeed—it is all stressful. Anxiety comes from fear. Fear that we'll fail. Fear that we can't cut it. Fear that trying will just prove that everyone's been right about us all along...

The truth is, everyone can learn. Everyone can improve. Everyone can achieve. Most of the time, if you believe you can't succeed, it's because your past experiences have made it seem impossible. However, those past experiences don't mean you can't succeed now. If you failed in school, it doesn't mean you'll fail in learning.

It's important to understand that test anxiety is normal. A healthy amount of test stress can be good. Stress launches adrenaline, a brain chemical that can make a test candidate more alert. Stress can motivate you to succeed. On the other hand, too much test stress inhibits clear thought, creates fatigue, and reduces performance. Months of studying and practice won't help if you freeze or fall apart during a test. What's the right balance between a healthy and productive amount of test stress and the kind of anxiety that overcomes test candidates?

Test Anxiety Strategies

PREPARATION

Consider the two-part test required for a driver's license. Most drivers are able to quickly memorize the rules of the road a day or two before the 20-minute test and perform without a problem once the testing officer is in the passenger seat. What would happen to a driving candidate who never looked at the driver's manual or had never been on the road? Not only would this want-to-be motorist fail to perform, but there would be high anxiety in the driver's seat.

Practicing for any test is the best way to reduce test anxiety and perform well. Study and take practice tests to prepare yourself for what a test will really be like. You can't cram for a test in a few minutes. For a big test, a good strategy is to study for a few weeks, a little bit every day. Then, take a practice test before you sit for the actual exam.

Practice tests prepare you by showing you what to expect. You'll be much more comfortable and confident if you understand what the test-taking process will feel like, and especially if you've succeeded on the practice tests. Practice tests teach test candidates how to use knowledge, provide testing experience, and are excellent indicators for measuring skill strengths and weaknesses. Practice testing also provides the best way to get familiar with the test structure, question and answer layout, and test timing and test expectations. Then, at test time, the test will be a known factor instead of an unknown factor. Test familiarity, along with knowledge ownership, helps candidates have confidence in their abilities and demonstrate their skills. These are prime strategies in reducing fear, overcoming test anxiety, and ensuring a solid test performance.

TIME MANAGEMENT

Time management can help reduce stress, not only for test-taking, but also for studying and managing your life. Making realistic time schedules relieves a lot of stress. Schedule time for classes, time for studying, and also time for rest. You need rest and relaxation in order to accomplish all your goals.

Many students express concerns about timed tests. Some may be slow test takers; some don't have a feel for how to pace themselves through the test. Test problems easily distract others—they concentrate on a few problems and answer well but find they're soon out of time and can't complete the whole test. Other test candidates may rush through the test because of time concerns—while they finish test sections quickly, they later learn that their answers were incorrect. There's no score or reward for finishing first or finishing fast.

You can improve your time management through practice. Managing your time on a test means:

! Looking over the test before you start and making a test plan

! Going through the test and answering the easy questions first

! Going back to take your time on the more difficult questions

! Knowing whether it's smart to guess if you can't find the right answer

! Keeping track of the time while you take the test

TIMING ON HSE TESTS

Timing varies for each different HSE exam and for each subtest. The full battery of tests includes science, social studies, math, reading, and writing. (On the GED® test, reading and writing are combined in one subtest.) On average, allow yourself about one and a half minutes for each question during practice test-taking and problem-solving to develop or improve time management skills. This strategy will serve to reduce test anxiety about timing and help candidates learn the art of pacing. On HSE tests, there's no penalty for guessing, so make an educated guess if you don't know the right answer.

Practice writing timed essays, as well. Allow 45 minutes to write a long response (or adjust your time for a specific essay test). Break up your essay time into time to think of an essay topic, time to prewrite and organize your ideas, time to draft the essay, and time to revise and edit the essay. If you've practiced beforehand, you'll do much better on the actual test.

PREPARING YOUR MIND AND BODY

While test candidates ensure that their abilities and time management skills are sharp, they'll also want to explore mental and physical ways to reduce test stress and incorporate stress reducers into their study program. Good nutrition, exercise, and healthy rest patterns are important. Knowing how to relax at test time is equally important; learn and practice relaxation techniques during long study sessions.

Know the Cues: Test anxiety doesn't just happen. It happens on cue. For many test candidates, anxiety is a habit. Just like the anxiety response is learned, it can be unlearned or shifted to a level where anxiety works for the test, instead of against it. Here are some typical test stress cues and strategies to manage them:

? Feeling overwhelmed? Take it step by step. Read directions carefully. Skip questions that seem overwhelming and move through another part first. Then return.

? Nervous and jittery? Test burnout halfway through? Avoid processed foods and fast foods, along with snacks and beverages with high-sugar content. Avoid caffeine. Try a banana or some green tea before a test.

? Feeling tense? Stiff neck? Eyestrain? Change positions. Stretch. Breathe deeply. Rest your eyes. Clear your mind. Start afresh.

? Blank? Frozen? Fearful? Relax. Skip the question and go to the next one. You're in control. You're ready, and you're doing your best. Take the test at your own pace, and the pacing you've learned and practiced will come back to you, along with the knowledge in your vault.

? Test fatigue? Eat a healthy snack. Use relaxation techniques. Pause. Clear your mind. Give yourself positive reinforcement. Visualize the goal.

? Just a little anxious? Expect it. Surrender to it. Even welcome it. Know that some anxiety can help you perform, provide energy, and increase thinking clarity. Acknowledge test stress as a further reminder of the importance of your goal. Make it work for you.

Answering Your Negative Thoughts

ADVICE FROM MOTIVATIONAL COACH VICKI HANNAH LEIN

We all make excuses for why we can't do things. There are lots of excuses why you "can't" get your HSE diploma. Here are some common negative thoughts that people face and ways to counter them.

"I don't have time, I'm too busy working."

You know how a pedometer works? It counts every step you take. All those little steps add up! Studying for an HSE exam is just the same. If you spend just 15 or 30 minutes a day doing lessons, you'll be amazed and proud of how much progress you can make and how quickly you can do it. You can make time for 15 or 30 minutes a day, and probably you can make more time than that. Remember, this extra effort is an investment in your future, and you can make it enjoyable. Studying doesn't have to be a chore. Make your studying interesting to you, and you'll actually learn faster.

"I've been out of school too long. I'll never learn this stuff!"

You already know most of what you need to know to pass an HSE exam, and you can develop a lot of other skills quickly. How long it takes will depend on when you left off school, what you've been doing since then, and how long it's been. It's doable for everyone, and it doesn't have to take that long. With the right study program, you can get back on track quickly and easily. Time passes faster than you think, and once you get going, if you track your progress, you'll see that you're moving toward your goal.

"I'll never pass the math!"

Most math tests require primarily basic everyday practical math. Tried and failed? Don't worry. You can learn it, if someone explains it to you in simple language you can understand and relate to real life! If what you've done in the past hasn't worked, don't give up. Try something new. Find the program that works for you. With the right study program and individual help if you need it, anyone can learn the math on an HSE math test. Part of learning math is taking it step-by-step, one piece at a time. Each part builds on the last thing you did. Even people who never thought they could do basic math can master HSE math.

"I can't get started."

Taking the first step is often the most difficult. Look at it this way…what do you have to lose? Getting started is all about making a commitment to yourself and starting to take the first steps. Once you're started on the road, it'll be easier to keep going. You'll be glad when you get to your goal!

"I can't afford the cost of a study program/the HSE exam."

Most HSE exams aren't that expensive, and neither are HSE study programs. A diploma gives you an opportunity to make a lot more money in the future. The investment is worthwhile. Most of the time, when people talk about not being able to afford an HSE exam, I find that what they really mean is they're afraid to try and fail. It's not that they don't have the money. It's an excuse to give up before they start. Don't let fear hold you back! If you really don't have the money, find a way to put it aside. Make it a priority, an investment in your future.

"I'm not a good reader/writer."

Reading is important for HSE exams, but it's also important for your life. You can become a good reader! The key is to start reading. Start reading every chance you get—and read something you'll enjoy. It's a rewarding way to spend your time.

Writing is also a skill you can learn, and it's easier than you think. Writing an essay is a learnable skill. Knowing what the HSE readers expect is half the battle!

When you're studying, find programs like the GED Academy™, TASC Prep Academy, or HiSET® Academy prep program that will give you audio input when you have to read. That will also help improve your reading quickly.

"I hate tests!"

I have taught thousands of people a few simple secrets that will change the way you take tests forever. This may sound like bragging, but when you take a test with the attitude, "I'm going to nail this sucker!" you'll be delighted to see how well your brain works and how good you can feel. Confidence breeds success.

"I started but stopped. I can't stick with it."

I understand. It's easy to lose momentum and get sidetracked. One thing that works for lots of people is to start with the easiest tests first. Nothing motivates you like success, and every test gets you closer and closer to your HSE diploma! You won't get there if you don't start… so take the first step!

Making a Motivational Study Space

Put motivational signs around your workspace to give you motivation to move forward every day. You can use the following motivational sayings, quotations, and reminders as decorations for your workspace. Even better, make your own motivational signs and decorations.

! Use pictures that remind you of what you're striving for and the rewards you hope to gain from your efforts.

! Use photos of your kids and your family, the people that you're trying to help by improving their lives.

! Don't forget yourself! Include photos of yourself.

! Find motivational quotes that speak to you and post them around your work area.

! Post a new sign marking every important goal you pass.

! Get your family and friends to write motivational notes for you to post in your work area.

Motivational Quotations

"God helps those who help themselves." —Benjamin Franklin

"The big question is whether you are going to be able to say a hearty yes to your adventure." —Joseph Campbell

"Destiny is not a matter of chance; but a matter of choice. It is not a thing to be waited for; it is a thing to be achieved." —William Jennings Bryan

"I'm a great believer in luck, and I find the harder I work, the more luck I have." —Thomas Jefferson

"When you reach the end of your rope, tie a knot in it and hang on." —Thomas Jefferson

"A man cannot be comfortable without his own approval." —Mark Twain

"Courage is resistance to fear, mastery of fear—not absence of fear." —Mark Twain

" Nobody will believe in you unless you believe in yourself." —Liberace

" The greatest danger to our future is apathy." —Jane Goodall

" Nothing is particularly hard if you divide it into small jobs." —Henry Ford

" Though no one can go back and make a brand new start, anyone can start from now and make a brand new ending." —Carl Bard

" I am not discouraged, because every wrong attempt discarded is another step forward." —Thomas Edison

" The human brain is unique in that it is the only container of which it can be said that the more you put into it, the more it will hold." —Glenn Doman

" Life engenders life. Energy creates energy. It is by spending oneself that one becomes rich." —Sarah Bernhardt

" Always bear in mind that your own resolution to succeed is more important than any one thing." —Abraham Lincoln

" If we attend continually and promptly to the little that we can do, we shall ere long be surprised to find how little remains that we cannot do." —Samuel Butler

Motivational Reminders

! I am doing this for myself.

! I am worth the effort.

! I am doing this for my family.

! Nothing ventured, nothing gained.

! It is possible to achieve success.

! It is possible to achieve happiness.

! It is possible to achieve prosperity.

! I am doing this for the rewards it will bring me. Thinking long-term will bring more happiness.

- I am taking responsibility for my life and going where I want to go.

- I can always be better and do more.

- Other people, with bigger problems than me, have done greater things.

- In the past, people may have told you that you're dumb or stupid, but ignore those voices. Everyone can learn. Everyone can achieve.

- I can prove to myself that I'm smart and worthwhile.

- Every day, I'm one step closer to success.

- My happiness is worth investing my time and effort!

- I am succeeding.

- I am making my own destiny.

- The more I do, the easier it gets.

HSE Exam Motivation

- An HSE diploma isn't something that's given to you. It's something that you earn.

- A half million people get an HSE diploma each year, and you can too.

- The HSE exam is the gateway to making hundreds of thousands—or even a million—more dollars in my lifetime.

- It will feel great to earn my HSE diploma!

- HSE graduates can do well in college and technical schools. I can get into college and become anything I want to be.

- An HSE diploma is required for more and more jobs each year. It's my best route to a better job or a promotion.

- Getting my HSE diploma shows my children that I value education. My children will do better in school if they see me succeeding with my education.

- An HSE diploma will allow me to help my children with their school.

- An HSE diploma will make me more confident in myself.

! An HSE diploma will show me that I'm capable of learning.

How I'll Overcome My Negative Thoughts:

HSE Success Stories

Here are just a few stories among the half-million people who get their HSE diploma each year. Each person has his or her own obstacles and problems and overcame them to be successful. You can, too.

Augustine's Story

I just want to encourage everyone who is about to take the next step… I, like many, received my HSE diploma, and I'm a perfect example of the advantages of earning a diploma. I'm currently in my junior year in college with a 3.95 GPA, tutoring other (high school graduate) students in college algebra.

The reason why I left high school was because my dad needed help with starting his own business and he needed help with the business. Although sometimes I feel like I should have stayed in school, the two years of experience in the real world helped me mature and think differently. Now I thank God for directing me through his path, a path that has not been easy but has opened doors to a bright future.

I got my HSE diploma to start my college education. Currently, I'm a student finishing my pre-requisites needed for the PharmD. (Doctor of Pharmacy) degree. My goal is to one day graduate, open my own pharmacy, and be an example to other young people like me. The only way my dreams will become reality is through the direction and help from God.

Remember, never give up… It is never too late to change your life.

Danielle's Story

Hi, my name is Danielle and for a long time I felt like I didn't have a name or identity. I really did not know who I was or where I was going. I was stuck in a dead end job paying minimum wage, and I was afraid to explore other opportunities because I didn't finish school or get my HSE. It was hard because I was out of school for 12 years. I forgot everything and had to learn all over again, but practicing and studying really helped me. In science I got 520, reading 560, writing 520, social studies 480, math 500 [high passing scores on a previous version of the GED® test], yes I am so happy!

I left school because I got pregnant and was on bed rest. I did not go back after I had the baby. I got my HSE diploma because I wanted a better life, I wanted my family to be proud, but most of all I wanted to prove to myself I am smart and I can overcome any obstacle with GOD at my side.

Don't ever let no one tell you that you can't. I am proof "yes you can," don't give up and when things get hard, and they will, remember you are worth it!!

Bradley's Story

I just got my HSE diploma on 11/29/07. My graduation ceremony will be 5/22/08. I also graduated with honors and won a $1000.00 scholarship. I will be attending Forsyth Tech. Community College in June. I will be taking Industrial Engineering classes and hope to one day own my own Electrical Business or Construction Company. I wish everyone good luck in getting their HSE diploma. Your program helped me to get mine with honors and a scholarship too. Good luck everyone!

David's Story

With the help of your program, I received my last test score yesterday and PASSED MY HSE EXAM! I could have never done in without your program.

I am 45, and was laid off after 20 years in the printing industry. I was offered a new job, in a new field, on the condition I got my HSE diploma. No small feat at this stage in my life. They were actually holding the job for me! The pressure was on! And OH how the testing and entire process has changed! I studied relentlessly, with much difficulty and frustration at times, as it's been a long time since I was in school and everything is ten times harder now.

Without your online tests and great study book, it would have taken me 6 months to a year to go to classes and learn at a snail's pace. I completed the tests and passed in a little over 1 month!!!! They are still holding that new job for me and I start next week.

Not having my diploma has always bothered me and held me back from taking new chances and changing my life for the better. Thank you so much. You've helped to increase my confidence, gotten me interested in reading again—it's overall changed my life!

Michelle's Story

When I was in 3rd grade the doctor diagnosed me with ADHD. My mother refused to let me take medication for my ADHD. I struggled every day until the end of 9th grade I just gave up. I refused to go back to school. I didn't understand the point of going to school.

I am now 27 years old, and I received my diploma on the 17th of January 2008. One of the most proudest days of my life. Throughout the years I tried several times to get my diploma but I gave up. For years people told me I couldn't do it, I was worthless. So I began to believe it and then slowly began telling myself the same things.

Until approximately 4 months ago I went back on welfare after losing another crappy job. They made me go to full time HSE classes. Two years prior to that I had passed my science and social studies test, so I only had three tests left. I started classes in November 2007, I decided to put all my effort and time into educating myself. I brought home the books and forced myself to learn the information in the books.

On January 16th 2008 I took my math test and received the results on the 18th that I had passed. That was one of the happiest times in my life. I have more confidence in myself now, and I will be enrolling into college in the fall. I view my future through a different set of eyes now, and I am unstoppable.

I left school because I did not know how to manage my ADHD and was told I was stupid. But I got my HSE diploma to prove to myself I was worth a better life. My goal was to get my diploma by the end of January 2008, and I have accomplished that. Then I will be enrolling in to college for a degree in Criminal Justice.

Don't give up on yourself, and life is what you make of it……..

Jeffrey's Story

I am an ex-convict who passed his HSE test at the age of 40. I am now enrolled at the University of Minnesota majoring in Human Resources. I was 18 years old in 1979 when I dropped out of high school. I want to finish my college degree in 2011. To anyone who reads this, pick up your diploma now.

Chimanga's Story

I was having a tough time in school because I made the mistake of associating with gang members. I left school in the 10th grade, because I wanted to hang out with my friends. I earned my diploma in 1992 at the age of 18. Dreams become reality through dedication.

I received my diploma 2 months after my 18th birthday, and I am really proud because I did so without anyone telling me to do it.

Mary's Story

Well, my name is Mary, and I am 19. I am married, and plan on going to college sometime to become an R.N.… It is my dream. When I was younger I struggled with social anxiety and depression. It was very hard for me to go into a crowded loud school, and so I started homeschooling.

I dropped out of school my sophomore year because I decided to move in with my boyfriend at the time. We met on the Internet, so I moved from OH to NY. I did homeschooling my 9th and 10th grade years but then got a letter in the mail at home that said each student would be required to come into the school on a bi-weekly basis. Since I could not do that, being in a different state and all, I decided to drop out. I do regret some of my past decisions, but I am happily married to that man now, and I love him very much.

I had always wanted to accomplish getting my diploma. It was important to me and to my family. Both of my parents dropped out of high school but then they got their HSE diplomas. When I was younger, I was in gifted and talented classes, even getting to go on yearly trips to historical sites in places like PA, and VA. When I decided to drop out of school my parents felt like it was a waste of potential, but I could not bear the thought of going back. Finally, after the age of 19, which is the legal age to take the HSE exam without some kind of consent in New York State, I decided to pursue my dream. I took the test on March 7 and 8, 2008. I eagerly awaited my test results. I got them today! I passed! I am looking at my diploma and the sense of pride that filled me brought tears to my eyes. I cannot recommend it enough. It is a scary position to be in, but I promise you will have no regrets. It is so very worth it. I scored an even 3000, my best score [730] in Language Arts—Reading.

I now plan on going to a community college to become an R.N.

Anything else in my life that would complete it in some way would have to deal with me becoming a nurse, preferably in a maternity ward. I love children and am empathetic.

My Motivational Thoughts:

_____

_____

_____

_____

_____

_____

_____

_____

_____

_____

_____

_____

_____

_____

_____

Motivational Worksheets

Use the following worksheets to help keep in mind why you're trying to accomplish your goals, to deal with obstacles when they come your way, and to keep yourself motivated. You can reach your goal!

My Notes

I Am Proud That:

1. _____

2. _____

3. _____

4. _____

5. _____

6. _____

7. _____

8. _____

9. _____

10. _____

11. _____

12. _____

13. _____

14. _____

15. _____

These Are the Good Qualities

THAT WILL HELP ME ACHIEVE MY GOAL:

1. _____

2. _____

3. _____

4. _____

5. _____

6. _____

7. _____

8. _____

9. _____

10. _____

11. _____

12. _____

13. _____

14. _____

15. _____

By Sticking to My Goal,

I WILL EARN THESE REWARDS:

1. _____

2. _____

3. _____

4. _____

5. _____

6. _____

7. _____

8. _____

9. _____

10. _____

11. _____

12. _____

13. _____

14. _____

15. _____

The People I Am Doing This for Are:

1. _____

2. _____

3. _____

4. _____

5. _____

6. _____

7. _____

8. _____

9. _____

10. _____

11. _____

12. _____

13. _____

14. _____

15. _____

The Reasons I Am Doing This Are:

1. _____

2. _____

3. _____

4. _____

5. _____

6. _____

7. _____

8. _____

9. _____

10. _____

11. _____

12. _____

13. _____

14. _____

15. _____

Obstacle Worksheet

Difficulties and obstacles are part of success.

On the road to my success, I've hit an obstacle.

I take responsibility for my action, and I'll get through this obstacle.

I will not let it stop me.

The obstacle is:

_____

I feel:

_____

_____

So far, what I've done is:

_____

_____

_____

I plan to:

_____

_____

_____

I WILL KEEP TRYING BECAUSE I KNOW THAT EVERY OBSTACLE IS ONE MORE STEP TOWARD MY SUCCESS.

Signature _____ Date _____

My Learning Contract

MY GOAL IS _____

    ! I pledge to work each day toward my goal.

    ! I take responsibility for my own success.

    ! I will not give up on my goal.

    ! I will remember all the good things that will come from my goal.

    ! If I fall behind, I will start working toward my goal again immediately.

    ! I won't let failing be a habit.

    ! I will get help when I need it.

    ! I will accomplish this for myself because I deserve it.

Signature _____ Date _____

Certificate of Achievement

Name: _____

Date: _____

I have achieved:

_____

I am responsible for this accomplishment.
I put my mind to it.
I worked hard.
I earned it.

Chapter 5

Test smart

How to Be a Successful Test-Taker

"I didn't fail the test, I just found 100 ways to do it wrong."

—Benjamin Franklin

Testing Smart

Many students have problems taking tests, even if they know the material. "I'm bad at tests" is a common complaint. This often comes from past experiences: test anxiety, poor grades, and multiple frustrations. Those past experiences are in the past, though. Test-taking doesn't have to be a frustrating obstacle.

A test is an opportunity. To take advantage of the opportunity, you need skills: test-taking skills. Like any other skills, you can learn how to be good at taking tests, and you can raise your score through better test-taking skills. That doesn't mean you don't need knowledge, but the combination of subject knowledge and test-taking skills will ensure success. Good test-taking skills can make a huge difference in your score. They give you an opportunity to show your knowledge!

If your goal is to pass an HSE exam, then test-taking is an important skill. Understanding the TASC test, HiSET® exam, and GED® tests is the first step. The more familiar you are with the test, the better you will do. Learning about the exam and applying basic test-taking skills will increase your confidence and boost your score.

A common problem with testing is that students might know information or have skills, but the test itself is too intimidating, confusing, or difficult to let them show what they know. Instead of being hampered and held back by the test itself, if you're a good test-taker, you can show what you know. The test will reflect your abilities in the subject being tested, instead of your difficulties with tests. That's why having test-taking skills is so important.

Familiarize Yourself with the Test

The first step in becoming a good test taker is getting familiar with tests. The more comfortable you are with tests in general, the more it will help you, especially if you're planning on moving on to college courses. You already know a lot about tests. You probably realize that:

! Most tests are timed, so it's important to watch your own progress during a test. Keeping track of time during a test is a skill that you can practice and learn. You'll read more about it in the section on How to Manage Time while Taking a Test.

! On most tests, you'll know in advance what's on the test in general, so you can be prepared for the test. Check out *Learn Smart: Secrets to Learning More in Less Time* to improve your ability to prepare.

! Most tests require you to read and write, but tests require specific reading and writing skills that you can improve, like reading directions, reading prompts, and writing essays. You can improve in these areas by taking practice tests that represent what you'll see on the actual test and learning more about the test you're taking.

! Different tests have different types of questions, and knowing more about the different types of questions helps you answer them correctly.

These might seem like simple observations, but they're fundamental to understanding how to be a successful test taker.

Understanding different types of test questions or tasks also helps you choose smart answers. A few types of questions include:

! Multiple-choice questions

! Drop-down menu question

! Short answer questions

! Show-your-work short answer questions

! Hotspot questions

! Drag-and-drop questions

! Essay or extended response questions

- True-false questions

- Matching questions

- Fill-in-the-blank questions

- Oral answer questions

- Diagramming/illustrating questions

- Performance tasks

- Identify parts of a whole

You can increase your confidence and your ability to answer questions by learning smart strategies to deal with specific kinds of questions. For example, a ***true-false*** test question seems straightforward. You're given a statement, and you need to decide if it's true or false. It's a myth that true-false questions are always easy, though. You need to really consider whether the statements are true or false, and sometimes they can be tricky. You can improve your ability to answer true-false questions by having a strategy to deal with true-false questions on a test. If you know a few things about *true-false,* then you can apply them to multiple choice as well.

- Words like "never" or "always" almost always make a statement false. Most of the time, statements that don't allow for exceptions (like *all* or *everything* statements) are false. Very few ideas are always true in every case.

  * On a multiple choice test, this applies as well... answers with "all," "always," "everything," "never," or similar words are usually wrong. At least, they should make you think. Is this really *always* true?

- Words like "sometimes" or "often" can be cues that a statement is true. Most of the time, statements that allow for exceptions (like "generally" or "usually" statements) are more likely to be true. Just look at the last two bullet points! I've used "almost always" and "most of the time" to indicate that there are exceptions to the rule... and many true statements on true-false tests will use similar sorts of words.

  * On a multiple choice test, this applies as well... look for answers with "sometimes," "often," "generally," "usually," or similar terms. These answers are more likely to be the correct ones.

❗ The whole statement will be false if any part of the statement is false. Read the whole statement and don't be confused by recognizing that *part* of what's being said is true. If you see anything that's not true, mark *false*.

✳ On a multiple choice test, you can use this rule, also. If part of an answer is untrue, that's not the correct answer... even if it's partially true!

❗ Don't let yourself get thrown off track by "no" or "not" words. Look for the words "no," "not," "cannot," "don't," or "can't." Throwing the word "not" into a sentence changes it from true to false or false to true. Make sure you catch those negative words so you're judging the right meaning.

✳ On a multiple choice test, the "no" or "not" might be part of the question. Look for statements like, "which of the following is **NOT** true..." and pay close attention to the "nots."

❗ Guess if you don't know, unless you'll be marked off for wrong answers. True-false tests tend to have more true answers than false answers. Why? It's harder to make up a false answer than a true one. If you're guessing:

✳ Follow your instinct first. If you have an idea, go with it.

✳ If you have no idea, guess "true." On a multiple choice test, this rule doesn't apply. You know there's one true answer and several false ones. You can still guess, though. Start by eliminating wrong answers to narrow down your guessing, and then always choose the same way from the remaining choices (such as the top answer or bottom answer) if you need to guess.

A multiple-choice question is just a series of true-false questions, and that's why many of the *true-false* answer techniques apply. You need to find the one true answer among four other false answers. There will be more tips on approaching multiple-choice questions in *Answer Smart: Thinking Through Test Questions and Answers*. When you're preparing for a test, it's best to prepare with questions as similar to the ones you'll face on the test as possible. Learn how to deal with the test questions, and you'll be one step closer to acing the test.

The HSE Tests

For a specific test like the GED® test, HiSET® exam, or TASC test, you want to understand beforehand what kinds of questions will be asked, how much time you'll have... in short, you want to know what it will be like to take the test. Here are breakdowns of what's on these three HSE exams.

GED® Test	
GED® Science	
Mostly multiple choice questions	Life Science 40%
Includes 2 short answer questions (about 10 minutes each), plus some fill-in-the-blank, drop-down, drag-and-drop, and hot spot questions	Physical Science 40%
	Earth and Space Science 20%
About 36 questions, 1 hour, 30 minutes	
GED® Social Studies	
Mostly multiple choice questions	Civics and Government 50%
Includes drop-down, drag-and-drop, fill-in-the-blank, and hot spot questions	U.S. History 20%
	Economics 15%
1 Extended Response (25 minutes)	Geography and the World 15%
About 36 questions, 1 hour, 30 minutes	
GED® Mathematical Reasoning	
Mostly multiple choice questions	Quantitative Problem Solving 45%
Includes drop-down, drag-and-drop, hot spot, and fill-in-the-blank questions	Algebraic Problem Solving 55%
	Includes an on-screen calculator for most items
About 46 questions, 1 hour, 55 minutes	
GED® Reasoning Through Language Arts	
Mostly multiple choice questions	Covers reading, writing, and language
Includes drop-downs (mostly language) in passages, drag-and-drop questions, and fill-in-the-blank questions	Informational texts, including science and social studies 75%
	Literature 25%
1 Extended Response (45 minutes)	Extended Response: Compare and analyze two texts
About 48 questions, 2 hours, 20 minutes	

HiSET® Exam

HiSET® Science	
50 multiple choice questions 1 hour, 20 minutes	Life Science 50% Physical Science 29% Earth Science 21%

HiSET® Social Studies	
50 multiple choice questions 1 hour, 10 minutes	History 38% Civics/Government 38% Economics 18% Geography 6%

HiSET® Mathematics	
50 multiple choice questions 1 hour, 30 minutes	Numbers and Operations 19% Measurement/Geometry 18% Data Analysis/Probability/Statistics 18% Algebraic Concepts 45%

HiSET® Language Arts—Reading	
40 multiple choice questions 1 hour, 5 minutes	Literary Text 60% Informational Texts 40% Covers comprehension, inference and interpretation, analysis, and synthesis and generalization

HiSET® Language Arts—Writing	
Part I—Multiple choice 50 questions 1 hour, 15 minutes	Organization of Ideas 25% Language Facility 41% Writing Conventions 34%
Part II—Essay 45 minutes	1 Essay, graded on Development of Ideas, Organization of Ideas, Language Facility, and Writing Conventions

TASC Test	
TASC Science	
48–49 multiple choice questions (1 technology-enhanced on computer) 1 constructed response item 1 hour, 25 minutes	8 Stimuli (passages or graphics) Physical Sciences 36% Life Sciences 36% Earth and Space Sciences 28%
TASC Social Studies	
48–49 multiple choice questions (1 technology-enhanced on computer) 1 constructed response item 1 hour, 15 minutes	8 Stimuli (passages or graphics) US History 25% World History 15% Civics and Government 25% Geography 15% Economics 20%
TASC Mathematics	
42–43 multiple choice questions (1 technology-enhanced on computer) 11 gridded-response (free entry) 1 constructed response item 1 hour, 45 minutes	Numbers and Quantity 13% Algebra 26% Functions 26% Geometry 23% Statistics and Probability 12%
TASC Reading	
48–49 multiple choice questions (1 technology-enhanced on computer) 1 constructed response item 1 hour, 15 minutes	Up to 8 passages Informational Texts 70% Literary Text 30% Vocabulary Acquisition and Use (10 to 15%)
TASC Writing	
50–51 multiple choice questions (1 technology-enhanced on computer) 1 essay based on two passages (45 minutes) Total 1 hour, 45 minutes	Writing 15% Grammar/Usage 30% Capitalization/Punctuation/Spelling 25% Knowledge of Language 30%

You'll see several types of questions on HSE exams. Most questions are multiple choice, which means you'll be able to pick one answer from a list of possible answers. This gives you test-taking advantages. You only have to recognize the correct answer, instead of calling it up from memory. You can eliminate incorrect answers, and you can guess. On HSE exams, you don't lose any points for marking an incorrect answer, so you should answer every question, even if you have to guess. Multiple-choice questions aren't the only ones on HSE tests, though. In addition, HSE exams have:

Essay or extended response questions: Each HSE exam has its own format for essay or extended response questions.

* The GED® test has two extended response questions in RLA and social studies. You'll need to write a short essay, maybe 4 to 6 paragraphs. (Aim for 250 words, aside from quotations.) You'll need to read passages and organize and communicate your thoughts about them. You'll need to cite evidence and have a main idea, a beginning, middle, and end. The GED® test also has two short response questions in science. These are shorter and test whether you can design an experiment and understand/cite evidence from a scientific text.

* The HiSET® exam has one essay question where you will have to write an argument. In 2016, the HiSET® exam will add passages. You'll need to read the passages and cite evidence from them in your response.

* The TASC test has one essay question, where you'll need to read a passage and write about the passage, citing evidence. The prompt will either be argumentative (so you will have to take a position about an issue and support it, citing evidence), or it will be informative (so you will have to describe something related to the passage and support your ideas/information with evidence).

Technology-enhanced questions: The GED® test and TASC computer-based test both include technology-enhanced questions. That can mean dragging and dropping a word or picture into the right place (drag-and-drop), clicking on a portion of a photo or a spot on a graph (hot spot), using a pull-down menu to select an answer (drop-down), or just typing in a single-word or single-number answer (fill-in-the-blank). Technology-enhanced questions make you answer the question in a different way, so that you're thinking about the question in a new way. Try to get some practice with technology-enhanced items before the test.

HSE exams include questions about a lot of topics, such as U.S. history and life science and sentence structure. However, that's not the only way the questions are defined. The questions on HSE exams are carefully chosen to include:

- Questions that include pictures, charts, and graphs, as well as text to read

- Questions that test thinking skills including knowledge, comprehension, analysis, application, synthesis, and evaluation

- Questions about important concepts behind the subject areas, such as technology questions on a science test

The best way to prepare for the HSE test experience is by taking practice tests, which recreate the experience of taking a particular HSE test. You don't need to jump into a full, timed practice test first. Working up to a practice test gives you more familiarity and prepares you to succeed.

- Start by walking through several practice questions to get familiar with what the test questions are like. Why are the questions structured the way they are? What are the questions asking you to do?

- Take an untimed practice test. Take as long as you need. Familiarize yourself with the test format and structure. Practice the whole test, including the essay.

- Use your practice test results to study. Time yourself for practice questions while you study, and try to work your time down to about 1 minute, 30 seconds to answer a question. (Some tests have shorter amounts of time per question, and some are longer. You can adjust your time for your particular test.)

- Before you take an HSE exam, take a timed practice test. Taking practice tests will improve your score on an HSE exam, even if you already know you're ready to pass. It's a simple step that can have great benefits.

Here's a practice question to get you started.

Science Practice Question

A man is camping at the ocean, and he wants to see if he can remove the salt from some of the ocean water. Which is the best way to get the salt that's in the ocean water?

1) Boiling away the water over his campfire

2) Heating the water in a closed container

3) Pouring the saltwater through a coffee filter

4) Pouring the saltwater back and forth from one cup to another

5) The salt cannot be removed.

Let's take a look at this question. It's a multiple choice question, like most of the ones on HSE exams, and it has five answers. The goal is to decide which of the five answers is true. The question talks about a man camping at the ocean. What's it really asking, though? The point is, how do you separate out salt from water? Whether it's ocean water or not, whether you're at the beach or not, that's extra information. The idea is, if salt is dissolved in water, how can you get the salt out of the water?

Have you got any experience with this type of situation? Have you ever gotten salt from water? Can you think of a way to get the salt out of the water? If you can, you're one step ahead.

If you can't think of an answer, it's no problem. You've got five choices to consider.

Answer 5 says that the salt cannot be removed. Well, that's a "not" statement. The salt **cannot** be removed. That seems pretty final. It's what is called an *absolute*. There's no room for an exception. That doesn't seem right, and it's not. That's an easy answer to eliminate.

Answer 4 is pouring the saltwater back and forth from one cup to another. Try to picture doing that. What happens? The water sloshes back and forth. Does any salt come out? What about other things combined with liquid? Say, fruit punch made from a powdered drink mix. Once you stir it together, would the punch mix come out if you poured it back and forth? Comparing the question to things in your life helps you put the answers in perspective. This one doesn't sound too likely.

Answer 3 is pouring the saltwater through a coffee filter. Do you think the salt would get stuck in the filter? What about the punch? If you poured punch through a filter, would you get a filter full of punch mix? You might not be sure, but it seems at least unlikely that all the salt or punch mix would come out. Think of making coffee. You put the grounds in the coffee filter, and the water pours through. On its way the water *picks up* coffee. It doesn't leave stuff behind in the filter. Water with something else in it (like coffee) can go through the filter just fine.

Answer 2 says to heat the coffee in a closed container. Try thinking of punch, or even coffee, again. If you heat it up inside a covered pot, does it separate, or does steam accumulate on the lid, turn to droplets, and drop back into the water? This one also doesn't seem likely.

Answer 1 is boiling the water *away* over a campfire. When you're done, the water's gone. What about the salt? Try thinking of the other examples. What if you put coffee in a pan and boiled it away? Would there be something left in the pan? What about punch? Would it leave residue behind? You've probably burned down some sort of liquid over the stove. The water goes away, burned off into steam, and it leaves behind—something. If it's saltwater, it's probably going to leave behind salt. This answer makes the most sense.

By thinking through the answers, you can try to eliminate ones that might sound right at first and come up with an answer that makes the most sense.

Why Do We Have Tests?

Let's talk about a really fundamental question. What's the purpose of a test, anyway? Why do we have them? Many students find tests annoying. They're difficult. They take time and effort. They don't seem to relate to real life very well. You might wonder why we have tests at all.

Tests have different purposes:

! Assessment—that is, to figure out what you do and do not know, so you can figure out what you need to learn.

! Placement—to put you into the program or level of study that's right for you.

! Diagnostic—to show where you have trouble and where you need help.

! Achievement—to show whether you've learned what you set out to learn.

! Qualification—to make sure you have the skills you need to advance into a college, a class, or even a job.

Simply, tests are a way to understand what you know. It's hard to quantify "how much you know," so teachers and organizations use tests to translate your knowledge into numbers—grades—that show what you know. Well, the system isn't foolproof. Some people do well on tests because they understand the test-taking process well and are able to express themselves well on a test. Other people freeze up when they take a test, or they have problems reading and writing, or they just have problems sitting still through a long test, and so they can't tell what they know. The good news is that it's possible to overcome these test-taking problems, and it's important because tests are necessary. They're the only way that institutions like colleges and employers can try to understand how much you know. It's not perfect, and it shouldn't be the only way learners are evaluated. Still, tests are necessary, and they're not going anywhere.

Common Test-Taking Problems

"I already know I'm going to fail."

If you've had bad experiences in the past, you might "know" that you can't pass, but bad experiences in the past don't govern your future. By becoming familiar with the test, practicing, and studying, you can succeed. You might be surprised at how easily and quickly you can pass. "Knowing" you're going to fail is a self-fulfilling prophecy. Try knowing that you'll succeed. Your attitude can make a huge difference!

"I'm so worried about the test that I can't concentrate."

If your mind wanders and begins to worry, try relaxation exercises. Before you start on the test, take a deep breath. Relax your body. Focus on one question at a time, trying to lock out anything else. Make the task small, instead of big. You can answer one question. Keep answering one question, and you'll be done before you know it. If you find yourself worrying, set down your pencil, take a deep breath, and refocus.

The more prepared you are, the less you'll worry, so study and take practice tests until you're confident that you can pass. Try taking one of the HSE subject tests at a time, if you can. Taking one test at a time will break the big task into smaller tasks.

"I freeze up. I know the material, but I'm too nervous."

You're aware of the problem. Good. Being a little nervous can be helpful, but being so stressed that you freeze up doesn't help! Practice taking tests in as realistic a situation as possible so that you can get comfortable in a test environment. The more familiar you are with sitting down and taking the test, the easier it will be to take the test. The more you think it's no big deal, the better you'll do! Worry and nerves are signs that you're not confident in yourself, so try to boost up your self-confidence.

❗ Remind yourself how well you've done on practice tests and in your studying.

❗ Know that the world isn't going to end, no matter what.

❗ Know that you have the ability to ace this test.

"I always run out of time."

Running out of time is a problem. You need to manage your time when you take a test. Read over the section on How to Manage Time while Taking a Test and be sure to practice timed tests before you take the real one. Practice makes perfect, and if you can do it in a practice test, you can do it on the real thing.

"Tests aren't fair."

Sometimes tests aren't fair, but examine your reasons for thinking it. Have you suffered from a teacher's badly worded questions in the past? All the questions on HSE exams are tested, and the ones that too many people get wrong are dropped from the test. Even if the people who wrote the question think it's fair, it doesn't matter. What matters is that a good amount of test-takers like you can answer it.

It's important to take responsibility for your own test score. If you say the test isn't fair, you're shifting the responsibility to someone else. The more you take ownership of your test score, the better you'll do, even when there are obstacles in your path. You'll be looking for solutions instead of letting someone else make you fail.

Some people feel tests are unfair because too often, they over-think the answers. The test questions aren't trying to trick you, so try to read the questions and answers in the most obvious way. Spend some time honing your test-taking skills. You'll soon find out that you can become a better test-taker.

"I can't sit still for a long test."

If you can't sit still for a long test, make sure that you take frequent breaks during your test-taking. Take a moment to catch your breath. There's usually no need to take all of the HSE subject tests at once, so take them one at a time. You'll perform better because you won't be too tired when you get to the next test.

If you feel you have symptoms of ADHD, talk to a doctor, and see if you can get diagnosed so that you can get help. If you've been diagnosed with ADHD, or have another documented disability, your testing center can provide special testing accommodations, such as frequent supervised breaks. Contact your local testing center for more information.

"I get distracted during the test."

It can be difficult to clear your head to take a test. Find a place to sit that's going to be least distracting for you, maybe near the wall so you're not surrounded by other students. Consider what's distracting you. Are you watching the other students? Looking out the window? Remove yourself from the problem.

What if you're distracted by worrying about the test? Worrying about how you'll do, what questions you'll get right, what time it is? Try practicing taking timed practice tests beforehand. It can help get you more comfortable with what you're doing. Also, try narrowing your focus while you're taking the test. Don't try to think about the whole test. That's a bit overwhelming! Think just about the question you're answering. Again, if you think you have symptoms of ADHD, talk to a doctor.

"I think I know the material, but I can't understand the way it's put on the test."

Practice with questions that are as close to the test questions as possible. You can learn to interpret the test questions so that you can understand them. You might need to learn some test-taking vocabulary so that it makes sense to you, and you might need to learn some strategies for understanding test questions. These are all skills you can improve! You can translate the questions into ideas that are more familiar to you and easier to understand. The more familiar you are with the actual HSE-type questions you'll find on the test, the more successful you'll be.

"The test questions are too tricky. I think one answer's right, but then I second-guess it."

If the test questions seem "tricky," you're probably over-thinking the answers. The questions are meant to be straightforward, so your first instinctive answer is more reliable. Don't look for a hidden meaning in the question's wording. Interpret everything in the most obvious way. People read into the questions because they're unsure of themselves. Be sure of yourself! You know more than you think!

The Day before the Test

So, you've done your studying, and you're ready to take the test. Your final preparation for a big test starts the day before the exam with a few simple steps.

Stop Studying.

Now's not the time to cram for the big exam. You might be tempted to take one last practice test, but stop yourself. Be confident in what you know. You've taken your time to study. It's more important to stop studying and take a rest. Let everything you've learned sink into your brain. Studying on the last day before the test is more likely to increase your stress.

Forget about the Test, Do Something Fun.

Do something to take your mind off the test tomorrow. Don't spend the day anguishing about it. Go out to a movie, or do something fun with your kids. You deserve to have a great day after the hard work you've put into preparing. Trust that you know what you need to know. It's the best way to spend the day.

Get Prepared.

The only thing you should focus on for the HSE exam the day before is getting together everything you need. Use the HSE exam prep checklist to make sure you're prepared. Put your clothes and everything you'll need together, so all you have to do is grab and go. Remember, the requirements will vary based on your state, so check with your local testing center about what you need to bring.

HSE Prep Checklist

Test Day and Time:_____

Test Site Location: _____

LEAVE PLENTY OF TIME TO GET THERE EARLY:

Time to Arrive:_____

Time to Leave Home: _____

ITEMS TO BRING

You may need these documents on your HSE test day. Check with your testing center to confirm which items you need to bring.

- ☐ Admission notice or test registration confirmation
- ☐ Driver's license, passport, or other picture ID
- ☐ Second form of identification
- ☐ Proof of residency
- ☐ Permission/exemption forms
- ☐ Previous test scores
- ☐ Social security number/card
- ☐ Payment
- ☐ Other:_____
- ☐ Other:_____

OTHER ITEMS TO BRING:

Check with the testing center to verify what items are allowed!

- ☐ Directions to the testing site/parking information
- ☐ No. 2 pencils
- ☐ Excellent erasers
- ☐ A small pencil sharpener
- ☐ Scratch paper

☐ An approved calculator if required or allowed. The GED® test allows you to bring a Casio FX260 handheld calculator to the math test, if you prefer it to the onscreen calculator. The TASC test preferred calculator is the Texas Instrument Model TI-30XS. Check with your test center for details.

☐ A watch (with no calculator)

☐ Ballpoint pen

☐ Reading glasses

☐ Water

☐ Healthy snacks or a lunch if you will have a break between parts of the exam (Good snacks include granola bars, cheese, bananas, apples, trail mix, nuts, or carrot sticks. Stay away from junk foods.)

☐ Extra money and change

☐ Tissues

☐ Layers of comfortable clothes to get comfortable in any room

☐ A book or magazine to read while you're waiting

☐ Other:_____

☐ Other:_____

REMINDER: YOU CANNOT BRING THESE ITEMS

Be prepared to leave these in the car or leave them at home.

☐ Cell phones

☐ Calculators (except those allowed by the test)

☐ MP3 players/music players

☐ Electronic organizers

☐ Pagers

☐ Study notes or books

☐ Rulers/compasses/measuring devices

☐ Any kind of computer or electronic device

Get a Good Night's Sleep

Well-rested test-takers do better. Don't drink any alcohol the night before the test. Instead, eat a healthy dinner and get some exercise during the day. Take a half-hour before bedtime to relax. Read, meditate, clear your thoughts. Envision doing great on the test and being relaxed. Get to bed early, and get a good night's sleep, a full eight hours, the night before the test. Your brain will function better, and you'll feel more confident!

My Notes

What to Do the Day of the Test

Test-taking day can be nerve-wracking. You're prepared. Relax. Be confident, and follow a few simple steps to do well.

Eat a Good Breakfast

You don't want to get hungry while you're taking the test. Eat a good, healthy breakfast that includes protein, carbohydrates, and fruits or vegetables. You'll have better concentration, more energy, and you'll do better. Here are some quick-and-easy breakfast suggestions:

- Have some oatmeal with milk, raisins, and fresh fruit, and a side of yogurt.

- Make a smoothie by blending up fresh fruits and a few veggies with some yogurt, and eat it with a bagel and cream cheese.

- Have a low-fat muffin with some yogurt and a banana.

- Make scrambled eggs with tomatoes, onions, and bell peppers, and serve it with a small bowl of cereal and fruit.

- Make hard-boiled eggs in advance, for a quick breakfast with toast, cheese or yogurt, and fresh fruit.

- If you don't like breakfast food, try a cheese and tomato or peanut butter sandwich with a side of fruit.

Don't Study!

Your studying is finished. Focus on getting to the testing center and taking the test. Anything you might learn at the last minute will be countered by the amount of stress last-minute studying causes.

Fill Your Spare Time

If your test is in the afternoon, find something relaxing and enjoyable to do to fill your time. Don't cram your day full of events, but don't leave a lot of spare time to fret. Choose activities that you can easily pick up and leave at any time.

Keep Track of the Time

Don't get caught up in something and leave late. You'll want to leave plenty of time and not have to rush out of the house or speed on the way to the testing center. Expect to arrive 15 to 20 minutes earlier than the suggested time. If you run into traffic or have problems finding parking, you don't want to arrive late and stressed. It's much better to have plenty of time to find the right location. If everything goes smoothly, don't spend the extra time worrying about the test! Relax. Read a book or magazine, or do a puzzle.

Go over Your Checklist

Make sure you have everything you need and that you know how to get to the test center. Check everything one last time before you walk out the door.

Think Positively

Positive thinking is the key to doing great on any test. Don't worry about not passing. Instead, wonder just how high your scores will be. Now is the time to feel confident. You're going to ace the test. No one has ever seen such high scores. If you feel a negative thought coming, just let it pass out of your head. Negative thoughts have never helped anyone do well on a test. Relax and be confident.

Starting the Test

Now that you've gotten to the test center and sat down with the test, where do you begin? Take a few minutes to get comfortable, look over the test, and make a plan before you begin. Planning, instead of jumping right in, is usually the key to success!

Choose Your Position

Take a desk or computer station that will give you as little distraction and as much comfort as possible. Try to stay away from the windows, doors, or aisles where there may be distracting movement. Instead, choose a well-lit desk in a central position, away from other test-takers if possible.

Get Psyched Up for the Test

Don't neglect your mood now that you're in the test room, ready to take the test. Give yourself a pep talk before you begin. This test isn't too difficult, and you're well prepared. You're going to ace it. Now is your time to succeed. Relax. You belong here. You want to take this test. It isn't a chore that you have to do. It's an opportunity for your future.

If the test room is cold, put on an extra layer of clothing that you brought. If it's hot, take off that sweater. You want to be comfortable. Settle your pencils and other things you might need during the test on the desk or in easy reach underneath it. Some testing centers won't allow you to have extra materials on your desk, so stow them underneath. Take out things that you might want and place them where they'll be easily accessible. Have your water at hand to take a drink. If you have any questions, don't be afraid to ask.

Finally, relax your muscles. Close your eyes and try relaxing each part of your body in turn, from your face, to your neck, to your shoulders, arms, wrists, fingers, back, stomach, hips, thighs, calves, and toes. Then stretch your limbs and find a comfortable position in your seat. You're ready to go!

Look Over the Test

Make sure that your name and any other necessary information is filled out correctly. You don't want any errors in your basic information.

Read the directions at the beginning of the test. Make sure you understand how to correctly select or mark your answers. If you have any questions, or if anything is confusing, ask the test administrator.

Glance over the questions in the test, noting how many questions you have to answer and how many selections you'll need to read. At a glance, do you recognize anything that you've been studying? Are there some questions that you know will be more difficult because of the pictures, charts and graphs, or long readings?

Looking over any test before you begin can be helpful. If it's a paper test, check fronts and backs of pages and make sure everything is clear to you. This is your time to organize your mind before you begin.

You may not be able to easily glance through an exam on a computer-based test; that's all right. You can scroll through the questions quickly if it's easy for you in the interface, or you can answer the questions one at a time. Look for a feature that lets you mark harder questions to come back to later.

Make a Plan for Your Test

Make a plan for answering the test questions. Many types of tests have different sections and different questions with different values. If you're taking this type of test, try answering the questions that are worth more first.

For multiple choice questions, all the questions have equal value. Each question is worth the same amount. A good strategy is to go through the test and answer all the easiest questions first. If a question is difficult for you, mark the question to come back to later. If you're taking a paper test, mark the number on scratch paper so that you can easily find it later. Make a note of the answer you think is right if you have a guess or an idea, but get all the questions you know the answers to out of the way up front.

Even on the easier questions, don't rush. Read through the entire question. Make sure you understand it before you answer or decide to wait until later. On your first pass through the test, you can mark guesses on a computer-based test, but not a paper-based one. If you're taking a paper-based test, make sure you're marking the answer sheet in the right place, and mark clearly and neatly. You don't want to get lost and spend precious time figuring out which question you *meant* to answer, and you don't want to erase if you can help it. Although you can erase answers, they must be erased completely so that they don't confuse the scoring machine.

Once you've done a first pass through the test, it's time to go back through for a second round. You have the questions you still need to answer marked on the computer or in your notes, so you can move to them quickly. On a second look, you might suddenly realize that you know the answer after all, or you might look at your initial guess and realize that it's right. (You might even realize that you were making a simple mistake or misreading the question. Good job, you caught it!)

On each question, decide whether you can figure it out or whether you need to guess. If you think you can figure it out, give it a shot, but keep track of your time. If a question is just taking too long, use a guessing strategy to guess the right answer and move to the next question. Focus on what you know and what you can answer, not on what is a struggle!

Keep track of the time while you work so you don't get caught up in one question. The goal is not to get that one, difficult question right. The goal is to get as many right answers as possible. You don't want to run out of time and not be able to answer the questions that you can figure out in a minute or two.

Don't worry about what the other test-takers are doing. Focus on the test, and if you start to get tired, take a break. Set down your pencil or your mouse, stretch your arms and neck, and relax your eyes for a minute. You'll answer best if you're fresh.

How to Read Test Directions

It can be easy to skip over test directions, and you certainly shouldn't spend all your time with the directions! However, test directions do tell you exactly what to do. A good strategy is to get familiar with the requirements of your test before test day. What will the test look like? Is it on a computer, or is it a paper test? Besides multiple choice, what kinds of questions will there be? What will you need to do? What can you expect on the writing portion?

When you take a test, read the directions carefully. The good news is that on an HSE exam, you can know most of the directions in advance. The main directions should also appear on official practice tests. You can find out what is being tested, what kinds of questions you'll have to answer, and how long you have to take the test.

Here's something that's important to know: for HSE exams, you shouldn't skip any questions. There's no penalty for guessing on an HSE exam.

You'll have directions before the whole test and also directions before individual questions, including the essay or extended response. If you're taking a computer-based exam, the directions will give you information about using the computer interface.

Here is an example of directions from a HiSET® science practice test. You'll notice that it gives you a lot of test-taking advice:

Not obscure facts!

Know how to answer multiple-choice.

Directions

Know how to manage time with multiple questions about a reading or graph.

This is a test of your skills in analyzing science information. Read each question and decide which of the four alternatives best answers the question. Then mark your choice on your answer sheet. Sometimes several questions are based on the same material. You should carefully read this material, then answer the questions.

Time management advice!

Work as quickly as you can without becoming careless. Don't spend too much time on any question that is difficult for you to answer. Instead, skip it and return to it later if you have time. Try to answer every question even if you have to guess.

Mark all your answers on the answer sheet. Give only one answer to each question and make every mark heavy and dark, as in this example.

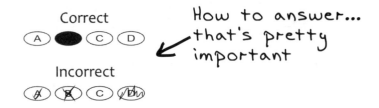

Correct

Incorrect

How to answer...
that's pretty
important

If you decide to change one of your answers, be sure to erase the first
mark completely.

Don't get
lost on the
answer
sheet!

Be sure that the number of the question you are answering matches
the number of the row of answer choices you are marking on your
answer sheet.

Source: HiSET Science Free Practice Test 1, available at http://hiset.ets.org/s/pdf/practice/science.pdf

These directions are pretty useful. Understanding them in advance will give you
a head start on the test. First, the directions tell you what the test is going to be about:
analyzing science information. That means you should practice thinking skills for
science: evaluating, inferring, and assessing science information.

You'll choose the best of four possible answers. That means it's a multiple choice
test, so be prepared with strategies to answer multiple choice questions.

Next, the directions say that you might need to answer more than one question
about a passage, graph, or other material. That is good information to know when
you're planning your time management. That's a lot of useful information in just the
first paragraph!

The second paragraph gives you some good time management advice. Work
quickly, but not so quickly that you're careless. If a question is tough, skip it and come
back later. Finally, guess if you have to! That's a good summary of time management on
an HSE test.

Next, it shows you how to mark the answer sheet. This part is only useful for
paper tests. On a computer, you'll click to select the right answer for a multiple choice
question. Also on a computer-based test, you won't have to worry about getting lost
and marking the wrong row on the answer sheet! If you're familiar with your test in
advance, you'll know how to plan and prepare.

What about a computer-based test? It's best to get some practice answering questions on a computer, including technology-enhanced questions, before taking the test. The GED® exam has a computer skills tutorial before the test. That's good, but it's even better to try the tutorial for free before you go to the test. You can find the tutorial and short free practice tests here: http://www.gedtestingservice.com/educators/freepracticetest

This tutorial goes over the **interface** for the test. An interface is all the things on the screen that help you understand and interact—buttons, scroll bars, menus, tabs. The tutorial also gives you examples of question types you'll see on the test: multiple choice, fill-in-the-blank, drop-down, hot spot, and drag-and-drop.

If you struggle with computer-based tests, get practice with computer learning before the exam. If you know in advance what you're dealing with, you have time to prepare! You can quickly become familiar with all the things you'll need to do on a computer-based test.

A lot of the test-taking advice for a computer-based test is the same as for a paper test. Don't spend too much time on a question. Manage your time. Don't leave unanswered questions, even if you have to guess. Your computer-based test will probably have a way to mark a question to come back to it later. That's useful! You don't have to take notes and spend time trying to find the question you didn't answer. Get familiar with the computer interface for your test. Find important features like how to come back to a question later. It'll save time when you take the test!

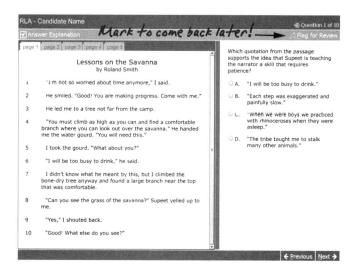

Source: GED® Reasoning Through Language Arts Free Practice Test Online, available at http://www.gedtestingservice.com/educators/freepracticetest

You'll also see directions for the essay or extended response portion of the test. Get familiar with what's expected before the test! Every HSE has its own requirements for writing and its own type of prompt. If you know what to expect on the test you're going to take, you'll do much better.

Here's an example of directions for a TASC essay test:

Before you begin planning and writing, read the two texts.

As you read the texts, think about the details from the texts you might use in your argumentative essay. You may take notes or highlight the details as you read.

After reading the texts, create a plan for your argumentative essay. Think about ideas, facts, definitions, details, and other information and examples you want to use. Think about how you will introduce your topic and what the main topic will be for each paragraph.

Now write your argumentative essay. Be sure to:

- Introduce your claim.

- Support your claim with logical reasoning and relevant evidence from the passages.

- Acknowledge and address alternate or opposing claims.

- Organize the reasons and evidence logically.

- Use words, phrases, and clauses to connect your ideas and to clarify the relationships among claims, counterclaims, reasons, and evidence.

- Establish and maintain a formal style.

- Provide a concluding statement or section that follows from and supports the argument presented.

Source: TASC Test Writing Practice Items, available at
http://www.ctbassessments.com/pdfs/TASC_WritingSampleTestItems.pdf

Whew! That's a lot of directions. They're easy to skip over. If you come to the test totally unprepared, they could be confusing or discouraging! These directions are most useful to you when you start studying and preparing. Why? They're a roadmap of everything you need to learn to write the TASC essay.

One important thing that these directions emphasize is the need to plan. You'll need to read, think about your essay, and decide what your main idea and details will be before you write.

Then, the directions give you a bullet-point list of everything that's in a good essay. If you follow all these directions and include everything in the bullet-point list, you'll do well! If you use this as a study guide and find out how to do every bullet point, you can write a great essay. When you take the test, the directions shouldn't be something completely new. They should be a reminder of everything you've learned—a checklist of what you need to do.

As you take the test, questions or groups of questions will include directions. Here's a direction that you might see:

Read this text. Then answer the questions.

or

Read this excerpt. Then answer questions 12–14.

or

Questions 2–6 are based on the information below.

Directions like these warn you that a passage (or chart, image, or other material) will be used for more than one question. When you're managing your time, think about these questions as a block of questions. It might take extra time to read the text or examine the chart, but you're using that time for two, three, or more questions. One good strategy is to briefly preview the questions before reading. That gives your reading purpose: you're reading to find answers and grasp concepts that you know you'll need.

Make sure you glance at all the directions. They might give you important information. You also can get important information from underlined, bold, or capitalized words in the question. Pay attention if the question contains a word like "not," "most," or "first." If the word is emphasized, the test writers are trying to help you get the question right. Figuring out which answer is NOT true is very different than figuring out the true answer. It can be confusing because it's easy to see one true answer, think "that's true!", mark it as correct, and move on without looking any further. Pay attention to words like "not" so that you don't rush past a question without understanding it.

Does the question ask for one "best" answer? If so, it says the one "best" answer, not the one "right" answer. That's the test writers being careful. You might say to yourself, "Well, this way might work, under such-and-such circumstances," or, "I don't know for absolute sure that this character would act in this way... maybe there would be some strange circumstance making them act another way." Because there are exceptions to (almost) every rule, the test writers want you to choose the one **best** answer to each question. That means, choose the most clear, straightforward, obvious answer if you interpret the question in the most straightforward way.

Taking Notes during the Test

During paper tests, you usually aren't allowed to mark the test booklet, and of course, you can't take notes on a computer screen (except on an essay). Still, it's important to make notes as you work so you can quickly go back to questions that you've skipped and also so that you can think through test problems. On some tests, the proctor may give you scratch paper to work out problems or take notes, and a paper essay test booklet should contain extra paper for planning your essay. Check in advance to make sure you can take scratch paper to the test center to take notes as you complete the test. Many test centers will provide you with scratch paper and don't want you to have your own scratch paper because it may contain notes.

If you have scratch paper, for a paper test, mark down the numbers of the questions that you need to go back and review. Mark your initial thought on the correct answer (for a computer test, you can select an initial thought or guess and change it later). Don't take a lot of time making notes, but make sure you have the information you need. If you have a question that's making you unsure, note it down. When you come back to the question, you'll have a new perspective. You may be able to see what wasn't clear the first time.

If you're not allowed to use scratch paper on a paper-based test, you'll still need to keep track of the questions you haven't answered. Be cautious as you mark answers on the answer sheet to be sure that you're marking the answer to the correct question. You'll know which questions to go back to because they'll be blank on your answer sheet. Do not try to lightly mark the answer sheet and then change it later, if you can avoid it, since this can cause the electronic reader to mess up grading your answer sheet. When you go back to the questions you skipped, try to jog your memory for your first-guess answer. If you're still unsure, your first guess is often right.

A computer-based test makes tracking your answers easier. You can usually enter your guesses and mark the questions to come back and check later. Make sure you're familiar with the computer interface before you take the test. Take a moment when you start the test to orient yourself and find the interface features you'll need. Do you still need to take notes? You'll need to work out problems, and sometimes planning on paper is easier and more effective than typing on a computer. Writing notes can help you think. Even if your test is computer-based, check with the testing center. Will they provide scratch paper? If not, are you allowed to bring your own?

Managing Time while Taking a Test

An HSE exam is a timed test, and running out of time is definitely something you'll want to avoid. Managing your time is something that you can learn. You'll know in advance how much time you have and about how many questions you have to answer. If you're prepared to manage your time, you'll get through all the questions and have the advantage of extra time.

Practice Managing Your Time

Like any skill, time management improves with practice. Be sure to take timed practice tests before you take the exam. Timed practice tests will allow you to improve your time management and make a plan that's right for you. Students usually have one of two problems with time management.

The first problem is running out of time. Maybe you spend too much time on tough questions. Maybe you get caught up in reading. Practice time management to make sure you answer all the questions you know first and at least guess on all the other questions.

The second problem is rushing through the test and not using all your time. Maybe you find tests frustrating or assume you can't answer the questions. Instead of taking a little time to think and check your answers, you guess or leave questions blank. When you take a practice test, use all your time. Practice reading and thinking about each question before judging whether you need to guess.

Have a Plan

As you're working on timed practice tests, start out with a plan. For example, on a 40-minute science test, you might decide that you'll take 15 minutes for the first run-through to answer the questions you know and then have 20 minutes left to go back and do the hard ones, with 5 extra minutes at the end. (Remember, most practice tests are half-length, so on test day you'll take twice the time.) If your timing doesn't work out, adjust it. Did it take you 20 minutes to go through the easy questions? 25? Can you improve that time? Did longer passages with multiple questions slow you down? Can you improve your time by focusing your reading on what you want to know or by skimming and scanning before reading? Based on your knowledge level and reading level, put together a timing strategy that will work best for you. Have your timing strategy ready before you go in to take the test. If there are too many hard questions, spend some more time studying and brushing up on your skills. Then try another practice test.

Watch the Clock

While you're working, you'll need to keep track of the time. Bring a watch that's easy to read at a glance, and be sure that it doesn't have a calculator or any extra features that might not be allowed at the test center. Don't use a beeping watch, since it will be distracting to the other test-takers and might not be allowed in the testing center. Practice beforehand with the same watch so you'll be comfortable and familiar with it. Note the times that you'll want to switch modes as you move through the test.

Some people have a good time sense and can tell whether 5 minutes or 10 minutes have gone by, and others don't. Practicing timed test-taking will help you better develop this time sense as you work so you won't be caught unaware without enough time to answer all the questions.

Glance at your watch frequently as you move from one question or question group to another. Develop this habit as you practice testing. This way, you'll always know how much time you have left, and you can update your time management strategy as you work. If you have scratch paper, you can write down the time the test ends and the time you should be done with your first pass through the section so that you'll have an easy reference.

Manage Your Time during the Test

If you've read the test directions in advance and completed practice tests, you'll know what to expect. It should only take a couple of minutes to review the test booklet or computer interface before beginning. You've saved time by being prepared.

If you've got a plan for answering the test questions, you'll be able to pace your movement through the exam. You'll have a good idea of how much time you can spend on a question before moving to the next one. You won't spend the same amount of time on each question because not all questions are equally easy or equally difficult.

During your first run through the questions, you'll spend much less time on each question. If you feel yourself getting stuck in a question and taking too much time, move on. Don't rush through the test questions, but take a reasonable amount of time to read carefully, think, and answer.

When you go back for the harder questions, decide if each is a 'must guess' or a 'think it through.' Be sure you've read the question correctly. If it's just something you have no idea about, don't spend a lot of time. Figure out your educated guess and move on. If you can think through the answer, do it. If you're getting bogged down and spending too much time, make your best guess and move on.

If there's a reading passage, don't just jump in and start reading blindly. Skim and scan to get an idea of what you need to read. Preview the questions to find out what you need to know. Then, read through the passage, looking for the answers and evidence you need. You might need to go back to the passage, but be smart about your reading time. Skim the passage to find the answer if it's appropriate for a question. Skimming and scanning long passages can save valuable time during the test. Read as much, or as little, as you need.

Take Breaks

Taking a lengthy exam can be grueling. Taking a couple of seconds to stretch your arms or your neck, to look away from the computer screen and relax your eyes, or to take a good, long yawn will make you work faster and save you time in the long run. Don't be so caught up in having to keep to your time schedule that you don't allow yourself a few seconds of break.

Use All Your Time

If everything goes according to plan, you'll have a few minutes left at the end of the test. Don't let that time go to waste. Read the section on Checking Your Test to make use of all the time you've got. Any improvement you can make to your answers gets you closer to your target score.

Staying Focused and Motivated

While you're taking the test, you'll need to keep your focus on what you're doing and keep yourself motivated. This is the most important time to keep your motivation level high.

Don't Let Difficult Questions Get You Down

There are lots of questions on an HSE exam. Some of them are tough. Expect that you won't know the answer to every question, and sometimes you won't have a clue! That doesn't mean you didn't study enough or that you won't pass the test. It's just the nature of the test. If you let the questions you don't know get you down, you'll end up spending too much time on them and feeling like you can't pass. The better strategy is to focus on the questions that you *do* know the answers to and thinking through the questions that you're not sure you know. Be prepared to guess when you don't know.

Don't Let Negative Thoughts Overwhelm You

While you're taking the test, take a vacation from any negative thoughts: worry about failing, pressure to do well, bad experiences with tests in the past. Let go of all of that. If it enters your mind, fine. Just let it flow right out again, just like it flowed into your mind. Don't latch onto it and worry. Many negative thoughts don't reflect reality, and if they're not useful, let them go. You've got a concrete task in front of you, to complete this one exam. Take it one question at a time and keep your attention on the exam. Trust in the preparation that you've already done. There's time to worry about everything else later!

Don't Second-Guess

Be confident in your test answers. Most of the time, your first idea is the correct one. Second-guessing your answers or your interpretation of the question is often the wrong move. You're over-thinking. The test questions are straightforward, and as long as you're not rushing and are reading the question carefully, you shouldn't have to second-guess. Don't spend your time worrying about the questions when you've already got the right answer. There are plenty of other questions to answer!

Don't Focus on Passing the Test; Focus on Taking the Test

You shouldn't be thinking too far into the future while you've got a test booklet in front of you. Yes, you're close to the end, and it's easy to start thinking about when you'll get your scores, whether you'll pass, what you'll feel like when...

Get rid of those thoughts.

There will be plenty of time after you've taken the test to plan, to wonder, and to sit on the edge of your seat waiting for the test results. Right now, you've got a job to do. It's a thinking job, but it's still a job.

Don't focus on passing the test. Focus on the test itself. You have to take the test before you can move forward to the next step. There's plenty to wrap your mind around in reading the test questions and making judgments on the right answers. It's a whole job, and it takes your whole mind. Give it your whole attention.

Don't Focus on Things around You

The other students and the proctor are doing their thing. You need to do your thing. The test booklet, the answer sheet, your scratch paper, and your watch should have 100 percent of all your focus. If you find yourself wondering who that guy or gal in the next row is, immediately look back at the question you're trying to answer. If you're glancing out the window, glance at your watch instead.

Do Take Frequent Breaks (and Bump Up Your Positive Thinking)

If you really can't focus or feel yourself getting tired, take a break of a couple of seconds. Clear your mind. Sometimes this can even help you approach the question with a fresh perspective and see the right answer. During your breaks:

! Don't worry or think about anything.

! Focus on physically rejuvenating your body by stretching, yawning, or relaxing your muscles.

! Take a sip of water.

! Give yourself positive thought-messages: You can pass the test. You're prepared. You've got a strategy.

! Go over your test strategy and your time management briefly, and make any adjustments based on the time.

! Get back to work quickly. You don't need more than a couple of seconds for a revitalizing break.

Do Keep Yourself Hydrated

Assuming water is allowed in the test center, take a sip of water whenever you need one. Don't drink a large quantity that will make you need the restroom frequently. A sip of water can wake you up and refresh you, but gulping down a whole bottle of water will mean interrupting your progress or being distracted by your bodily needs.

Do Eat During Your Breaks

When you have a test break, take the time to have a snack. You won't want to get hungry later, and now's your opportunity. Don't eat sugary, carbohydrate-laden junk food, like candy or cupcakes. Instead, bring fresh fruit, vegetables, granola bars, nuts, trail mix, and other healthy, fortifying snacks. Good snack foods will help keep you going and stop you from getting hungry during the test.

Checking Your Test

If you've managed your time well, you'll probably have a few minutes left at the end of the test. Make good use of the extra time.

First, make sure that you've answered all the questions and that the answers are correct on the computer screen or clearly and completely marked on your answer sheet. Don't skip any questions. If you find a missing answer, look at the question. If you know the answer immediately, great. If you're not sure, use a guessing strategy to give yourself the best odds of getting it right. Usually, you can eliminate at least one or two wrong answers to make your guess more likely.

Run quickly through the test to make sure that you haven't misread or misinterpreted any questions and to see if you have a sudden inspiration about a question that you just didn't get at first. Don't expect to do a thorough read! This is just a spot check in case you happen to see something that's wrong. Be wary of changing your answers, though. Don't let a second look become second-guessing. Most of the time, your first answer was the right one.

If you're sure you've made a mistake, change your answer. If you're taking a paper test, completely erase the wrong answer and fill in the correct answer choice. Be careful not to leave any marks that might confuse the electronic grader.

If you're taking a test that includes a constructed response or essay, read through your response for spelling and punctuation errors. You can make minor corrections or even add to your essay if you have a sudden inspiration. It's especially easy to add thoughts or make corrections on a computer-based test. If your test is paper-based, don't make a lot of confusing marks. Make minor corrections or add to your conclusion.

When time is up, take a deep sigh of relief. You're done! Go out and celebrate!

Chapter 6

Answer smart

Thinking Through Test Questions and Answers

"I think now that the great thing is not so much the formulation of an answer for myself, for the theater, or the play—but rather the most accurate possible statement of the problem."

—Arthur Miller

Answering Smart

Having a strategy to answer HSE questions is essential. Most questions on an HSE exam are multiple choice. You'll need to choose a correct answer based on reading text or looking at pictures, charts, and graphs. That means your reading skills are important, but different reading tasks require different skills. By focusing on developing reading skills to understand questions, passages, and answers, you can score better on your HSE exam.

Multiple-choice questions give the test taker an inherent advantage: they do not require precise knowledge to get the correct answer, but rather, the ability to choose the most likely answer or alternative from only four or five choices. You might know the answer right away without even looking at the choices. You might recognize the answer when you see it, or you might be able to narrow down the choices to one correct answer by thinking through the question and answer choices logically. Having choices to review is a big advantage on a test.

Don't misunderstand this to mean that you don't need to study and prepare for a multiple choice test or that an HSE exam is easy. It is not easy; it is a whole-day exam. HSE exams are normed to graduating high school seniors, and only a portion of those seniors can pass the tests. What the multiple-choice advantage means is that you can maximize your study time to focus on critical thinking and comprehension skills. You don't need to recall obscure facts or details, and with some strategic test-taking, you can increase your score.

How to Read a Test Question

The better you understand what the question is asking, the easier it is to answer the question. Read each word in the question and pause a moment at the end to absorb the meaning. Test creators design questions for clarity. They are not designed to test what you do not know, but rather, to demonstrate how you can interact with the material in the test. The questions are intended to make you think carefully and critically. They are for the most part straightforward and easy to grasp. ***The biggest reasons for getting the wrong answer are that the reader did not read carefully or did not follow directions.***

Essentially, the question is the key to the answer! By following a few simple guidelines, you can read and understand the test questions more effectively and be more likely to find the correct answer. Part of learning to read test questions is understanding how they're written and why they're written that way.

Test Questions Aren't Tricky or Cleverly Worded

The goal of test writers is not to find out if you can see through trick questions. The goal is to find out if you can answer straightforward questions that require certain skills. That's why test makers try out their questions on test-takers before they use them as real questions. Only questions that aren't too hard or too easy make it into the test. That should eliminate questions that are worded confusingly or rely on tricks. That's why test questions should be simple to understand. An HSE exam does not try to trick you or give you confusing questions. Read for the most obvious meaning of the question. Your first instinct about what it means is probably the correct one!

Check for Words Like "NOT"

There are some key words that can completely change the meaning of a test question. Take a look at this test question:

> Which statement is a fact, not an opinion, supported by the chart of Johnson Brothers' earnings?

The test writers are actually trying to help you out by putting "not an opinion" in the question to clarify that they're looking for a fact *as opposed to an opinion.* If you're not reading carefully, your eyes might skip over some of the words and focus on the word "opinion." If you're looking for an opinion in the answer choices, you'll choose wrong. It's important to carefully and completely read the test question.

Some tests try to help you out by putting the word "NOT" in boldface, underlining it, or using all capital letters:

> Which of the following is **NOT** a conclusion based on the above passage?

In this question, the word "NOT" completely changes the meaning of the question. If your eyes skip over it, you'll read "is a conclusion..." and you'll be looking for the wrong answer. It's a good reason to read all the answers to the question before choosing one. If you see more than one answer that seems right, go back and read the question again to make sure you read it correctly.

Another similar word to watch out for is "except." Take a look at this question:

> All of the following are examples given by the author, except:

The word "except" shows you that you need to look for the exception—look for the answer that is **NOT** an example given by the author.

Pay Attention to Bold or Underlined Words

The word "NOT" is sometimes highlighted in test questions, and other words can be, too. Take a look at the following example:

> Which is the <u>best</u> conclusion based on the sales chart?

The word "best" is emphasized because some of the answers *might* be conclusions from the sales chart. You'll have to read all the answers and decide which one is the best. Which one has the strongest evidence in the chart?

Here's another example:

> What conclusion could you come to based **only** on the sales chart?

This question is similar, but slightly different. The conclusions might be valid, but the question wants the one that uses information **only** from the sales chart. Watch out for answers that might use information from somewhere else! Notice that these words are included because the test writers want to make sure you understand the question. Take advantage of the help!

Look for Key Words

Key words in a question tell you important information about what the question is asking. Look for words like:

! *comparison, compare:* to show how two things are similar or different

! *conclusion:* an opinion or idea based on facts

! *consider:* think about

! *decrease, reduce, lessen:* to make smaller or have less

! *defend:* to give evidence for

! *describe:* to tell about, often restating what's in the reading

! *determine, produce:* to cause

! *evidence, basis, support:* the facts that support a conclusion, or show it's true

! *explain, explanation:* to give a reason for **or** tell what something means

! *increase, enlarge, gain:* to make bigger or have more

! *influence, affect:* contribute to or partially cause

! *most effective, most acceptable, most appropriate:* best

! *require:* need

! *shift:* change

! *similar:* like one another

! *suggest, imply, implication:* a conclusion based on the reading, picture, or chart

! *summarize:* to give the main idea

! *valid, accurate:* correct

Know What Types of Questions You'll Run Into

Y ou'll run into similar types of questions that use different wordings. Look at the following four questions:

> Which statement best summarizes the above chart?

> Which statement best expresses the main idea of the passage?

> What would be the best title for this passage?

> Which of the following statements most accurately describes the information in the chart?

Each question asks you to *summarize a main idea*. One asks for a summary of the information. Another asks about the main idea. The third asks for a title. The fourth asks for a statement that describes the chart. A summary, a main idea, a title, or an overall description of something are all similar. They all give the main ideas or central focus of something. No matter how it's worded, you're looking for a main idea. If you expect questions about summaries or main ideas, you'll know how to recognize them and what they're asking you to do.

Here are a couple of additional examples of questions worded in different ways that ask you to use the same thinking skills:

Skill	Example Questions
Telling facts from opinions	Which of the following is a fact, not an opinion, based on the above table?
	Which of the following is an opinion based on the information in the passage?
	Which of the following is a conclusion by the author included in the passage?
Recognizing facts that support a conclusion or recognizing a conclusion based on facts	Which of the following statements is best supported by the above chart?
	Which of the following is the best conclusion based on the passage?
	Which of the following facts provides the best evidence for this conclusion?
	Which of the following represents the most appropriate conclusion one might draw from this table?

The more you're familiar with the kinds of skills test questions require, the better you'll be able to interpret and answer the questions.

Restate the Question in Your Own Words

To make sure you understand the question, try restating it to yourself in your own words. What does the question really mean? What's it asking for? If you can understand the question, you're well on your way to choosing the correct answer.

Answering Multiple-Choice Questions

Once you understand what the question is asking, it's time to choose your answer. Let's take a look at finding the correct answer first, and then we'll go over a strategy for guessing if you're not sure of the answer.

Answer the question in your head before you look at the answers.

The multiple-choice answers can confuse you if you have not formed a sense of what is being asked before you begin to consider the choices. Sometimes two or three answers will be very close in meaning, and unless you have a good idea of what the answer should be before you look at the choices, you might waste valuable time. Take a few seconds to think about what the answer should be before you start looking at the answers listed in the problem. This may seem like an unnecessary step, but it will save you time in the long run and prevent choosing answers on impulse or having to go back and reread the answers a second or third time.

Look for the answer in the test.

Most of the questions on an HSE exam do not require knowledge outside what is given in the test. The questions require you to think and consider and then to choose an answer from the information given to you. They don't expect you to know a lot of facts and outside information beyond basic knowledge and familiarity with concepts. When you start looking for the answer, look in the reading, chart, graph, or picture on the test. That's where you'll find the answer.

The exam is testing your skills for finding, understanding, and drawing conclusions based on information, not being able to recall random facts. In general, don't look outside the test question for information. Only look at the information the test is giving you.

Some science and social studies questions are an exception. Still, pay careful attention to the information in the test. The details you need are there. You'll use basic knowledge to answer the questions, but you'll also use the information on the test.

Eliminate answers you know are wrong.

As you read the answer choices, you will encounter some answers that are obviously wrong. Eliminate those answers. This will help you narrow the choices, and it will make choosing the correct answer easier. The wrong answers won't interfere with your thinking if you've eliminated them.

If you have to guess, eliminating the wrong answers will make it much easier. Really think about it! You might find that you can eliminate all but one of the answers as wrong and know that the last answer is correct. It's possible to find the correct answer without necessarily knowing what it is. After eliminating the wrong answers, you might realize why the remaining answer must be true. It doesn't matter, though. When you eliminate a wrong answer, you're showing your knowledge. If you have enough knowledge to eliminate all but one answer, then you've demonstrate your knowledge of the skill being tested.

Go with your first answer.

Statistics from numerous studies have shown that a test taker's first choice is usually the correct one. Your brain told you this was the best answer first, so go with it. Don't go back and change your answer unless you have a very solid reason to do so. Remember, the HSE exam should be a straightforward test with clear questions. Trust your instincts.

If you don't know, guess.

Your score on an HSE test is based on how many questions you answer correctly. There is no point penalty for a wrong answer. Eliminate the obviously incorrect answers and take your best guess from what is left. In most cases you can eliminate two, sometimes three obviously incorrect answers. This leaves a 33% to 50% chance to guess right. Following are some guidelines for improving your guessing percentage.

Guessing Strategies

To compensate for the multiple-choice advantage for the test taker, test writers include answers that are designed to be plausible—that seem like they could be correct. Following are some strategies that you can use to see through these seemingly "correct" answers. The most common reasons you will miss correct answers are that you misread either the question itself or text that goes along with the problem, or you simply did not follow directions. Your first strategy is to read every question and answer carefully. Give each question and answer your full attention and focus. Read every word and make sure you understand exactly what is written.

When you read a multiple-choice question, there are three possibilities:

1. The first possibility is that you know the correct answer. You read the problem, and you can easily pick out the correct answer. Great!

2. The second possibility is that you definitely do not know the answer. You don't have a clue. That's fine. Guess.

3. The third possibility is that you are unsure of the answer. You have some idea, but you are not positive one way or the other.

The third type of question can hurt your score the most because you will tend to choose the answer that your hunch tells you is correct or you'll over-think the question and begin reading into it. These are the most confusing questions to answer, and so you need a solid strategy for answering them correctly. You'll need to think it through.

Another challenge is deciding if an answer is a #2, where you have no clue, or a #3, where you are unsure but might have a hunch. Hunches can defeat you. The reason hunches are so problematic is that the test writers have written answers that "look correct" but are not. Your "hunch" might just be a correct-seeming answer that's causing you problems. These answers appeal to the hunch-takers because they are in the gray area of sounding "kind of" correct.

Guessing Strategy #1: Kill the Hunch

Here's an easy way to test the correctness of your hunches. Ask yourself if you would bet $100 on your hunch. One hundred dollars is a lot of money to most people. You will probably not risk $100 on an answer that is just a hunch. The $100 betting strategy will help you decide if an answer is just a hunch, a guess, or actually based on some knowledge you have about the topic. Your goal is to eliminate the hunches and put the answer into the pure guess category, #2, or the #1 category, where you base your choice on actual knowledge and experience.

When you discover that your hunch is really just a guess, you put the answer into the second group (#2), the questions you do not know how to answer. Now you can take a guess without the influence of the hunch, and your chances of getting a correct answer are much better. The hunch answer was most likely wrong because the test writers put it in the test to make sure it wasn't too easy to come up with the correct answer through elimination. The test writers want to make sure you're thinking clearly, so the "misleading" answers are meant to weed out people who are just guessing. (You don't need to "just" guess... you can be successful with a good, thoughtful guessing strategy.) By eliminating the foggy hunch answer, you have increased your chance considerably. Now, you can use the law of averages to guess better and show that you're thinking about the answers, even if you don't know them all.

When you do not have a clue which of the answers is correct, you will want to make a purely random choice. Make a rule that you will follow whenever you encounter a pure guess choice, after you eliminate incorrect answers. An example is taking the last of the choices. Follow that rule in every single case. If you eliminate answers that you know are incorrect and follow a simple rule (instead of a hunch) to guess, you can get 30%, 40%, or more of these answers correct, depending on how many incorrect answers you can eliminate. That can be a big boost to your score.

Guessing Strategy #2: Eliminate Answers You Know Are Wrong

Read through all the answer choices. Chances are, you'll know that at least one of them is incorrect. If it doesn't make sense or is clearly wrong, eliminate it. Use your knowledge to increase your guessing success.

Guessing Strategy #3: Watch Out for Slang

You won't often come across slang or very informal language on a standardized test; this rule might be more helpful for less rigid test. Still, it's important to be aware when an answer is informal or sounds like slang. Answers that use slang are generally incorrect. Use a little caution with this rule because the inverse is not always true. Answers that are the most scientific and formal sounding often are correct, but not always. Test writers sometimes write answers that have a formal or scientific feel to them that are incorrect. That's to make the answers "sound" right when they're not really correct.

The strategy of eliminating slang answers is used to eliminate wrong answers, not necessarily to pick correct ones. Answers that use slang words will be wrong more often than not, so eliminating them increases your chances of choosing the correct answer. You may not find many "slang" answers on an HSE exam, but if you do, you'll know what to do with them.

Guessing Strategy #4: Extremes or Absolutes

Watch for words like *always, never, none, all, best, worst,* or *solely.* These words indicate absolutes or extremes, and correct answers rarely are absolutes or extremes. It's not very often that something is "always" or "never" true. In science, some physical laws may be "always" true, but even physical laws often depend on context. The law of gravity is constant, but gravity is different on Earth than on the moon. In general, avoiding "always" or "never" statements is a good idea. Just look at the test questions themselves. They say things like "which is the *most likely...*" or "what is *typically...*" They don't say "which one is *always...*" because there aren't many "alwayses" in the world. Answers with extreme or absolute words are usually incorrect. Eliminate them from your choices on principle, even though they may seem correct.

Choose answers that use qualifiers like: *sometimes, typically, generally, may, can, likely, could, often,* or *might.* These "sometimes" words show that there are possibilities for exceptions, and the world is full of exceptions! In a guessing situation, choices that use qualifiers will be correct more often than not. They will give you an edge when you do not have a clue.

Guessing Strategy #5: Opposites

If there are two answers that are opposites of each other, one is likely to be correct. It's often easy to create a wrong answer by turning around the right answer into its opposite, so you'll often see opposites on the test. Opposites can catch a test-taker who's not reading carefully or thinking it through well. When you find opposites, one of the two opposite answers is likely correct. You are now down to a 50/50 choice. If, by narrowing down your possible answers to two choices, you can put the question in the #1 category and make an informed guess about which one is correct, that's great! Still, be sure to apply your $100 bet to make sure you're not just using a hunch. If you don't know which answer is correct, the best strategy is to use your rule for guessing and move on to the next question.

Here's a summary of the guessing strategies.

1. First, use the $100 bet rule to eliminate hunches. Hunches will be incorrect more often than they are correct. If you do not feel like you could bet $100 on your answer, you will be better off statistically just taking a guess at it. Your answer should be based on a *logical reason* instead of a hunch.

2. Eliminate answers that you know are wrong based on your knowledge of the question and your critical thinking skills.

3. Eliminate answers that use slang. They will more often be incorrect than correct.

4. Answers that are absolutes are most often incorrect. You can eliminate these answers, too.

5. If a question has answers that are opposites of each other, the correct answer is most likely one of the opposites. If you cannot make an informed choice between your opposites, use your guessing strategy, such as choosing the last answer after eliminating incorrect answers.

6. Apply a consistent guessing strategy like always choosing the last of the choices, after eliminating wrong answers. Never deviate from the rule.

My Notes

_____
_____
_____
_____
_____
_____
_____
_____
_____
_____
_____
_____
_____
_____
_____

One Question May Help You Answer Another

During your test, you will skip some questions to answer later. It's possible that you'll run across another question later *that clarifies the first question.* For example, suppose you skipped the following science question:

Oppositely charged objects:

1) Attract

2) Repel

3) May attract or repel

4) Attract then repel

You might use a guessing strategy and say that "attract" and "repel" are opposites, and there's also the word "may" in answer 3. Maybe you're planning to guess between those three. Later in the test, you find the following question:

A positively charged object attracts an uncharged object. The positively charged object attracts the negative ions in the uncharged object, pulling them closest to the positively charged object and repels the positive ions. Based on this information, which statement must be true?

1) Ions don't have a charge until they come into contact with a charged object.

2) Negatively charged objects do not attract uncharged objects.

3) An uncharged object is made of positively and negatively charged ions.

4) A positively charged object attracts positive ions.

If you think this one through, the text says that the positively charged object attracts negative ions and repels positive ions in the uncharged object. Even if you don't know what ions are, you know that there are positive and negative ones in the "uncharged object." Answer 3 is correct.

There's more you can get out of this. If a positive charge attracts a negative charge, that means opposite charges attract. That gives you the answer to the previous question. It's one of the opposites—answer 1.

Now, when you don't know the answer to a question, there's no guarantee that there will be more questions on the same topic later, but if you see any, pay attention to them. They give you additional information that you could use.

Practice Questions

Practice your tactics for reading and answering questions with the following ten practice questions. Try for the correct answer first, but if you don't know it, use guessing strategies.

My Notes

_____

_____

_____

_____

_____

_____

_____

_____

_____

_____

_____

_____

Directions: Choose the <u>one best answer</u> to each question.

Science

Use the following diagram to answer <u>questions 1 and 2</u>.

The Electromagnetic Spectrum

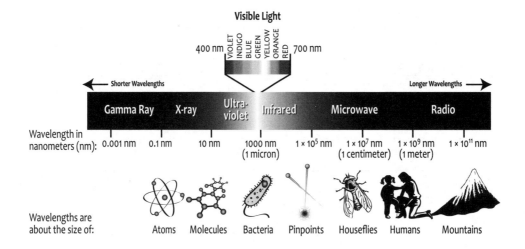

1. Based on the above illustration, most of the electromagnetic spectrum:

    1)   Is invisible

    2)   Has short wavelengths

    3)   Is visible

    4)   Has wavelengths the size of pinpoints

    5)   Cannot be measured

2. Which of the following is most likely the wavelength range of yellow light?

1)   340–380 nm

2)   420–460 nm

3)   550–590 nm

4)   630–670 nm

5)   780–820 nm

Social Studies

Use the following diagram and text to answer <u>questions 3 and 4</u>.

Supply and Demand

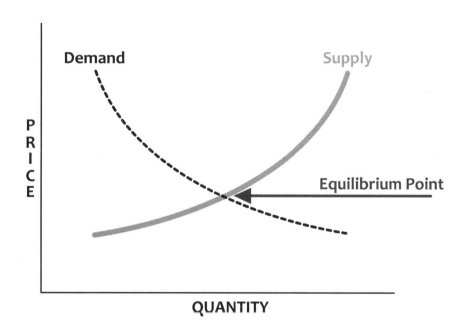

The principle of supply and demand states that in a free market, the price of items will be determined by the supply of those items and the demand for those items. At higher prices, demand decreases while supply increases. At lower prices, demand increases while supply decreases. The market price will be at the equilibrium point between supply and demand.

3. Which of the following situations is most likely to increase the price of the hottest new toy during the Christmas season?

   1)   The supply is low due to unexpected high demand for the toy.

   2)   The supply is high due to anticipated high demand for the toy.

   3)   The demand is low due to anticipated high supply of the toy.

   4)   The demand is high due to unexpected high supply of the toy.

   5)   The supply and demand are equal.

4. Which of the following statements best summarizes the principle of supply and demand?

   1)   The equilibrium point is where supply and demand meet.

   2)   Supply and demand move in opposite directions.

   3)   The price and quantity of a product determine its supply.

   4)   The supply of and demand for a product will determine its price in a free market.

   5)   At lower prices, demand goes up while supply goes down.

Reading

Use the following poem to answer <u>questions 5 and 6</u>.

WHAT SEEMS GOLD TO THE AUTHOR?

Nothing Gold Can Stay

1   Nature's first green is gold,
    Her hardest hue to hold.
    Her early leaf's a flower;
    But only so an hour.
5   Then leaf subsides to leaf.
    So Eden sank to grief,
    So dawn goes down to day.
    Nothing gold can stay.

Robert Frost, "Nothing Gold Can Stay," 1923

5. In the second line of the poem, the best synonym for the word "hue" is:

1)   Moment

2)   Leaf

3)   Feeling

4)   Sunrise

5)   Color

6. In lines 2 and 7, which literary technique does the author use?

1)   Apostrophe

2)   Alliteration

3)   Personification

4)   Metaphor

5)   Onomatopoeia

Writing

7. When <u>you decide, on a course of action</u> please notify me.

Which is the best way to write the underlined portion of this sentence? If the original is the best way, choose option (1).

1) you decide, on a course of action
2) you decide on a course of action
3) you decide, on a course of action,
4) you decide on a course of action,
5) you decide on, a course of action

8. With you're permission, we will finalize the plans for the library tomorrow.

Which correction should be made to this sentence?

1) Remove the comma after <u>permission</u>
2) Change <u>you're</u> to <u>your</u>
3) Change <u>library</u> to <u>Library</u>
4) Change <u>will finalize</u> to <u>have finalized</u>
5) No correction is necessary.

Math

9. A square patch of lawn has an area of 36 square feet. How much fencing would be required to completely enclose the lawn?

1)   12 feet

2)   24 feet

3)   30 feet

4)   36 feet

5)   72 feet

10. How many possible $9.99 dinner specials can be ordered off this menu?

You-Choose-It Dinner Specials, $9.99

Choose one appetizer, one main course, and one dessert.

Appetizers	Main Courses	Desserts
Buffalo wings	Grilled lemon chicken	Banana split
Quesadillas	Roasted veggie fajitas	Chocolate cake
Nachos	Spicy barbecue ribs	Apple pie
Cheese fingers	Steak and salad	Cherry-cheese pie
Double-up Appetizer for $1.99 More!	*Half-and-Half Main Courses for $2.49 Extra!*	*Double-up Dessert for $1.99 More!*

1)   12

2)   16

3)   32

4)   48

5)   64

STOP! Answer the Practice Questions Before Moving Forward

Practice Question Answers

et's take some time to walk through how to approach these different questions. Don't just check whether your answers were correct. Think about how you answered the questions. What thought process did you go through to get your answers? What techniques did you use? Even if you didn't get the correct answer, give yourself credit for weeding out incorrect answers and narrowing down your choices. If you got any guesses right, give yourself a pat on the back!

My Notes

Science Question 1

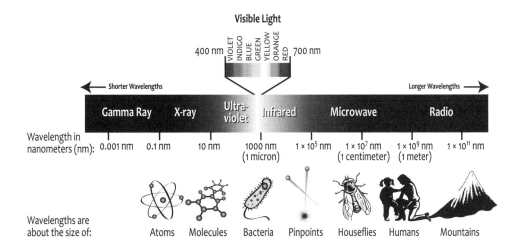

The Electromagnetic Spectrum

1. Based on the above illustration, most of the electromagnetic spectrum:

1) Is invisible ⟵ Correct!

2) Has short wavelengths

3) Is visible

4) Has wavelengths the size of pinpoints

5) Cannot be measured

When reading this question, it's important to pay attention to the keyword *most.* You want to know what quality applies to the largest part of the electromagnetic spectrum in the picture. Notice that the answer is contained in the picture. The test gives you all the information you need.

You might be able to answer this question by thinking about it carefully. Looking at the chart, it shows that a small amount of the electromagnetic spectrum is visible. Most of the electromagnetic spectrum is *invisible*. The answer is 1.

If you aren't sure, you can use guessing strategies to narrow down the choices. First, you might eliminate answer 5, "cannot be measured," because it's an absolute (canNOT). Still, you can do better than that. The answers contain two opposites, "is invisible" and "is visible." If you narrow it down to those two, you've got a 50/50 chance of being right. Narrowing it down to "is invisible" and "is visible" also may make it easier to pick out the correct answer. You can look at the graph and ask, "Is more of the electromagnetic spectrum *visible* or *invisible*?" You'll likely be able to see that most of it is *not* visible.

Science Question 2

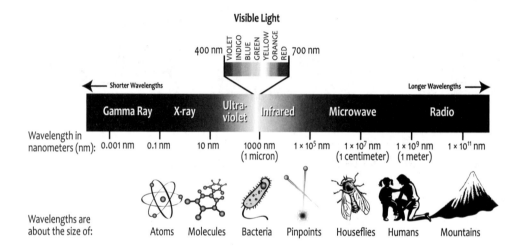

The Electromagnetic Spectrum

2. Which of the following is most likely the wavelength range of yellow light?

1) 340–380 nm
2) 420–460 nm
3) 550–590 nm   ← *Correct!*
4) 630–670 nm
5) 780–820 nm

This question asks you to look for yellow light in the diagram, but there's no specific wavelength measurements labeled "yellow light." That makes it a bit harder. You'll have to think about it. See if you can eliminate some wrong answers.

Yellow light is visible, since we see the color yellow. You can eliminate anything outside of the range of "visible." That means, anything that's not between 400 nm and 700 nm is incorrect. You can eliminate answers 1 and 5. If you did that, you've increased your chances of picking the correct answer to 33%, a big increase.

Now, you could think this through even more. The left side (400 nm) of visible wavelengths is labeled "violet." The right side (700 nm) is labeled "red." Yellow isn't at the far right or the far left. It's somewhere in the middle. The colors go: violet, blue, green, yellow, orange, red. Yellow is in the center, but a little closer to red.

That should eliminate answer 2. Answer 2 is very close to violet, and there needs to be blue and green before you get to yellow.

Now, there's two more answers, a 50/50 chance. Logically, answer 3 is more in the center, so you might realize it's correct. Even if you're not sure which answer to choose, if you've narrowed it down this far, you've greatly increased your chances of guessing correctly! Even if you didn't get your guess right, on a long test, the odds will be with you and will get you a better score.

Social Studies Question 3

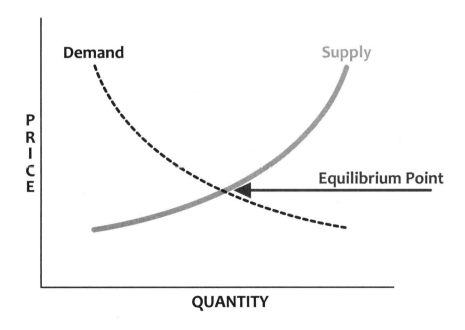

Supply and Demand

The principle of supply and demand states that in a free market, the price of items will be determined by the supply of those items and the demand for those items. At higher prices, demand decreases while supply increases. At lower prices, demand increases while supply decreases. The market price will be at the equilibrium point between supply and demand.

3. Which of the following situations is most likely to increase the price of the hottest new toy during the Christmas season?

    1)   The supply is low due to unexpected high demand for the toy. *Correct!*

    2)   The supply is high due to anticipated high demand for the toy.

    3)   The demand is low due to anticipated high supply of the toy.

    4)   The demand is high due to unexpected high supply of the toy.

    5)   The supply and demand are equal.

This question contains the keyword *increase*. It asks you which situation will make the price of the toy higher. If you understand the terms "supply," how much of something there is, and "demand," how many people want it, your common sense and experience will help you answer this question. Don't read too much into it or over-think the question! What causes the price of a toy to rise?

The first answer says that the supply is low (there are few toys) and the demand is high (lots of people want them). When many people want a few toys, the price goes up.

If you find that you need to guess, though, you're faced with an odd situation. There isn't just one set of opposites here. There are two! Answers 1, 2, 3, and 4 are all variations of each other, substituting "high" and "low," "supply" and "demand." You can probably eliminate answer 5, and that increases your chances of being right from 20% to 25%...a significant gain.

Could you eliminate any other answers? You might eliminate answer 3 because low demand is unlikely to cause high prices. (If people don't want something, why would they pay a lot for it?) That would give you a 33% shot at the answer.

Now, if you look at the answers carefully, you'll see that answers 2 and 4 both say there's high supply AND high demand. The reason is different, but the conditions are the same. When two answers are so similar, it's unlikely that either of them is right!

That could help you narrow it down to answer 1—so you *could* arrive at the correct answer in more than one way.

Social Studies Question 4

Supply and Demand

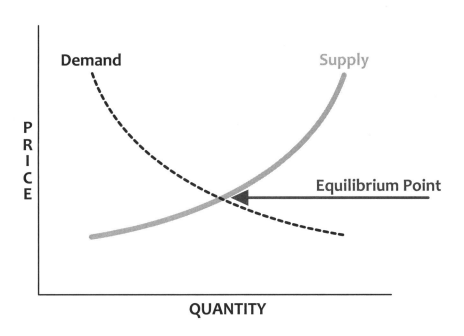

The principle of supply and demand states that in a free market, the price of items will be determined by the supply of those items and the demand for those items. At higher prices, demand goes down while supply goes up. At lower prices, demand goes up while supply goes down. The market price will be at the equilibrium point between supply and demand.

4. Which of the following statements best summarizes the principle of supply and demand?

    1) The equilibrium point is where supply and demand meet.
    2) Supply and demand move in opposite directions.
    3) The price and quantity of a product determine its supply.
    4) The supply of and demand for a product will determine its price in a free market.
    5) At lower prices, demand goes up while supply goes down.

Correct!

This question asks for a summary. That is, what's the main idea of supply and demand? Be aware when a question asks for a summary or main idea. Watch for answers that just give details. They may say something correct, but they won't be the right answers.

Answer 1 is exactly that kind of answer. It gives a definition of the equilibrium point, but that doesn't really give the main idea of the principle of supply and demand. It's true, but it doesn't sum up the whole idea. You might be able to eliminate this answer with a little thought.

Answer 2 is also true, but it also doesn't tell you what the main idea is of the principle of supply and demand. This one might be easier to eliminate because it doesn't really give an important point.

You might eliminate answer 3 as well, because the price and quantity of a product don't determine its supply. It doesn't say that anywhere in the text. Instead, the supply helps determine the price.

Now you've got two answers left. You could eliminate answer 5 because it only talks about lower prices. The principle of supply and demand talks about what happens to prices in general, not just about lower prices.

If you eliminated any of the incorrect answers, then you increased your odds of getting the right answer. Answer 4 is the best answer because it gives the main idea of what supply and demand is about: that supply and demand determine the price of items. Remember, in this type of question, you're looking for the broadest answer that gives the best overall idea of the topic.

Reading Question 5

WHAT SEEMS GOLD TO THE AUTHOR?

Nothing Gold Can Stay

1 Nature's first green is gold,
   Her hardest hue to hold.
   Her early leaf's a flower;
   But only so an hour.
5 Then leaf subsides to leaf.
   So Eden sank to grief,
   So dawn goes down to day.
   Nothing gold can stay.

Robert Frost, "Nothing Gold Can Stay," 1923

5. In the second line of the poem, the best synonym for the word "hue" is:

1) Moment

2) Leaf

3) Feeling

4) Sunrise

5) Color  *Correct!*

Here's a question that might be hard if you don't know the answer right away. If you know what "hue" means, you'll immediately see that 5 is the correct answer. What if you don't know? This is a common type of question on a reading test, a word definition question.

One good strategy for eliminating wrong answers is putting them in the sentence to see how they sound.

"Nature's first green is gold, her hardest *moment* to hold." That sounds like it might be right, so skip that one for now.

"Nature's first green is gold, her hardest *leaf* to hold." Well, the word "green" does apply to a leaf. It's hard to eliminate that one, either.

"Nature's first green is gold, her hardest *feeling* to hold." The thing that's being held refers to what's "green" and "gold." The word *feeling* doesn't make a lot of sense. You can probably eliminate answer 3.

"Nature's first green is gold, her hardest *sunrise* to hold." Well, "gold" might apply to a sunrise, but "green" likely wouldn't. The sentence doesn't really sound right. Later on, the poem talks about "dawn," but it doesn't really seem to apply very well here. You can probably eliminate answer 4. If you've eliminated two answers, you've got your chances up to 33%, pretty good odds.

"Nature's first green is gold, her hardest *color* to hold." That's the last answer. It's the most dead-on because "hue" is talking about what's "green" and "gold." Obviously, those are colors. Going with what's most obvious is usually best! You might go with this answer after thinking about it, but even if you didn't, you should be able to eliminate a couple of wrong answers!

Reading Question 6

WHAT SEEMS GOLD TO THE AUTHOR?

Nothing Gold Can Stay

1   Nature's first green is gold,
    Her hardest hue to hold.
    Her early leaf's a flower;
    But only so an hour.
5   Then leaf subsides to leaf.
    So Eden sank to grief,
    So dawn goes down to day.
    Nothing gold can stay.

Robert Frost, "Nothing Gold Can Stay," 1923

6. In lines 2 and 7, which literary technique does the author use?

1)   Apostrophe

2)   Alliteration   ⟵ — Correct!

3)   Personification

4)   Metaphor

5)   Onomatopoeia

This question is actually more difficult than most HSE reading questions because it requires that you know some literature terms. Most HSE exams don't test you on literary terms, but you might still find yourself up against some vocabulary words you don't know. If you know the answer, that's great. If not, you still might be able to eliminate some answers before guessing.

You might be tempted to eliminate "apostrophe" because it's a kind of punctuation. However, the word "apostrophe" also has a different meaning as a literary term. If you eliminated it, that's okay. You've got to go with what you know. Remember, test writers try to make their answers sound right. You might assume that "apostrophe" is a kind of literary technique you don't know. Actually, "apostrophe" means talking to some idea, force, or character directly. An example would be if the poem said, "Oh, Nature, you cannot hold the color gold!" That's talking directly to Nature.

Check for terms that you know. You're most likely to know "personification" and "metaphor." If you know that "metaphor" means calling one thing a different thing to draw a parallel (like saying, "Her early leaf's a flower," which calls the leaf a "flower"), then you'll see that there isn't a metaphor in lines 2 or 7. You can eliminate answer 4.

You might be thrown by "personification," though. "Personification" means treating something that's not a person (like nature) as a person. Line 2 calls nature "her," which is a type of personification. It treats nature as a woman. Still, there's no personification in line 7, and if an answer is only partially true, then it's false! You can eliminate answer 3.

You might not know what answer 5 means. "Onomatopoeia" is a word that is patterned after a sound. A good example is "woof," which sounds like the noise a dog makes, or "cock-a-doodle-do," which is supposed to mimic the sound of a rooster. Answer 5 is incorrect, but you might not be able to eliminate it.

The correct answer is 2, "alliteration." Alliteration means having words that start with the same letter. In line 2, the words "hardest," "hue," and "hold" all start with the same letter. In line 7, the words "dawn," "down," and "day" all start with the same letter. If you didn't know the term "alliteration," this might be a really hard one to get right. If you eliminated any wrong answers, you did a good job!

Writing Question 7

7. When <u>you decide, on a course of action</u> please notify me.

Which is the best way to write the underlined portion of this sentence? If the original is the best way, choose option (1).

1) you decide, on a course of action
2) you decide on a course of action
3) you decide, on a course of action,
4) <u>you decide on a course of action,</u> ← *Correct!*
5) you decide on, a course of action

The writing questions can sometimes make it hard to eliminate wrong answers. You won't come across many opposites or absolutes to give you clues. This question asks you to decide on the best way to write part of a sentence. All of the choices have to do with commas. Can you eliminate any wrong answers?

When you're doing a question about commas, try reading through the sentence with a pause where the comma is:

> **When you decide [pause] on a course of action please notify me.**

You might be able to eliminate the original sentence (answer 1) because it sounds wrong.

If the comma sounds wrong after "decide," you can eliminate answer 3, too. Adding an extra pause doesn't make it sound right:

> **When you decide [pause] on a course of action [pause] please notify me.**

Now, you're down to three choices. Answer 2 doesn't have a comma at all:

> **When you decide on a course of action please notify me.**

It might be difficult to eliminate that one, so keep it in mind. Answer 4 has one comma after "action":

> **When you decide on a course of action [pause] please notify me.**

That should sound okay, too. The last answer has a comma after "on."

> **When you decide on [pause] a course of action please notify me.**

That one probably sounds wrong, and you can eliminate it. That brings you down to a 50/50 chance, which is great odds.

If you know the rule to put a comma after a dependent clause (clauses starting with words like "when," "since," or "because") at the beginning of a sentence, you'll know that answer 4 is correct. If not, you've done well to eliminate some incorrect answers and improve your chances of getting it right.

Writing Question 8

8. With you're permission, we will finalize the plans for the library tomorrow.

Which correction should be made to this sentence?

1) Remove the comma after <u>permission</u>

2) Change <u>you're</u> to <u>your</u>   ← ⎯⎯ *Correct!*

3) Change <u>library</u> to <u>Library</u>

4) Change <u>will finalize</u> to <u>have finalized</u>

5) No correction is necessary.

Here's another writing question. This one isn't only about commas, though. It has a lot of choices. The problem might be a comma, or the commonly misspelled word "you're," or capitalization, or a verb, or no correction at all. All of them are common types of mistakes.

Can you eliminate any incorrect answers? You likely can eliminate one or maybe two of them. It depends on what kind of punctuation, spelling, and grammar knowledge you have. You can try reading the sentence with and without a pause after "permission" to see if you can eliminate answer 1:

> **With you're permission [pause] we will finalize the plans for the library tomorrow.**

> **With you're permission we will finalize the plans for the library tomorrow.**

If both sound okay, leave them as possibilities. The pause might sound a little more natural than without the pause, so you may be able to eliminate this answer. Removing the comma is not the best answer.

Answer 2 is the right answer, but you might not know it. "You're" and "your" are commonly confused. You can't tell the difference in how they sound, but you can tell if "you're" is right by substituting "you are" into the sentence:

> **With you are permission, we will finalize the plans for the library tomorrow.**

Clearly, "you are" is wrong. That means "you're" is misspelled, and answer 2 is correct. If you don't know it, you'll have to move on and check out the other answers.

Answer 3 changes "library" to "Library." The only way to eliminate this wrong answer is if you know that the word "library" by itself should not be capitalized. It's only capitalized if it's part of a name, like the Benjamin Franklin Memorial Library or Library of Congress. If you know the rule, you can eliminate this answer.

Answer 4 changes "will finalize" to "have finalized." You can probably eliminate this answer by reading aloud to yourself what the change would sound like:

> **With you're permission, we have finalized the plans for the library tomorrow.**

"Have finalized" is in the past, and "tomorrow" is in the future. It sounds wrong because the times are wrong. This answer can be eliminated.

The answer "no corrections are necessary" is hard to eliminate unless you can spot the right answer. Hopefully, you should be able to narrow down your choices at least by one!

Math Question 9

9. A square patch of lawn has an area of 36 square feet. How much fencing would be required to completely enclose the lawn?

1)   12 feet

2)   24 feet ⟵――― *Correct!*

3)   30 feet

4)   36 feet

5)   72 feet

This question requires you to read it carefully and picture in your mind what it's really asking. It's an easy one to misunderstand! You might have a "hunch" that the answer is 36 feet, since the number 36 is the only one in the question. For the same reason, you might have a hunch about 72 feet, which is 2 times 36. Well, throw your hunches away on this one!

To think it through on math problems, drawing a picture on your scrap paper can definitely help.

The **square** is **36 square feet** in **area** (that means, the size of the inside of the square), and you're looking to **enclose** it with a **fence.** That means the number you *want* is around the outside of the square, the distance around the edges.

You've gotten this far. Can you eliminate any of the answers? Yes, you can probably eliminate 36 because the perimeter (around the outside) is probably not the same as the area. You can probably eliminate 72, too, because it seems too high. You also might eliminate 12 as too low, based on the 36 square foot area. That leaves 24 and 30 feet.

The trick to solving this is to find out how long one side of the square is. The area of a square is one side times another side. Since both sides are the same, the area is one side squared: side². What number, times itself, is 36? In other words, what's the square root of 36? The answer is 6. The amount of fencing would be 6 + 6 + 6 + 6, or 24.

Here's another way you might think about it. The square has four equal sides. The fence is probably evenly divisible by 4 to make the problem easily solvable. It's got to be in 4 equal pieces. If you've narrowed the answer down to 24 and 30, you can eliminate 30. Each side would have to be 7.5 feet, and the area would be 7.5 × 7.5, which is more than 36. If the answer is 24, then each side is 6 feet, and the area would be 6 × 6, or 36, which is correct. Even if you can't eliminate the largest and smallest numbers by estimating, you can eliminate them using this process.

Math Question 10

10. How many possible $9.99 dinner specials can be ordered off this menu?

You-Choose-It Dinner Specials, $9.99
Choose one appetizer, one main course, and one dessert.

Appetizers	Main Courses	Desserts
Buffalo wings	Grilled lemon chicken	Banana split
Quesadillas	Roasted veggie fajitas	Chocolate cake
Nachos	Spicy barbecue ribs	Apple pie
Cheese fingers	Steak and salad	Cherry-cheese pie
Double-up Appetizer for $1.99 More!	*Half-and-Half Main Courses for $2.49 Extra!*	*Double-up Dessert for $1.99 More!*

1) 12
2) 16
3) 32
4) 48
5) 64 ← Correct!

This question has some extra information: the prices for extras to the dinner special. If you recognize that you can ignore the extra prices, you're ahead of the game. The question is, how many $9.99 (no add-ons!) dinner specials can you order?

It might be tempting to eliminate the highest and lowest number on principle, but unless you have something to estimate from (like the area in the previous question), don't be tempted. That's a "hunch"!

There are three columns to choose from and four choices in each column. A random guess is better than going with a hunch like 4 × 3 (12). Think it through... are there more than 12 choices? Well, you can make 16 different dinners with just Buffalo wings, without using the other appetizers. If you spend a little time going through counting dinner choices, you'll realize there are a lot more than 12.

You might be able to eliminate 16, too, by counting, but you would spend too much time if you tried to count to determine all the choices.

If you realize that 64 is 4 × 4 × 4, you might recognize it's the right answer, because it makes sense to multiply all three columns together to get an answer. If not, you'll have to guess! If you were able to eliminate any of the answers by thinking it through, you're increasing your chance for a high score.

My Notes

"A civilized man is one who will give a serious answer to a serious question."

—Ezra Pound